Workshop Towards a Formal Distributional Semantics 2013

Held at the 10th International Conference on Computational Semantics (IWCS 2013)

Potsdam, Germany
19 March 2013

ISBN: 978-1-62748-400-8

Printed from e-media with permission by:

Curran Associates, Inc.
57 Morehouse Lane
Red Hook, NY 12571

Some format issues inherent in the e-media version may also appear in this print version.

Printed by Curran Associates, Inc. (2013)

For permission requests, please contact the Association for Computational Linguistics
at the address below.

Association for Computational Linguistics
209 N. Eighth Street
Stroudsburg, Pennsylvania 18360

Phone: 1-570-476-8006
Fax: 1-570-476-0860

acl@aclweb.org

Additional copies of this publication are available from:

Curran Associates, Inc.
57 Morehouse Lane
Red Hook, NY 12571 USA
Phone: 845-758-0400
Fax: 845-758-2634
Email: curran@proceedings.com
Web: www.proceedings.com

TABLE OF CONTENTS

Semantic transparency: challenges for distributional semantics

Melanie J. Bell
Anglia Ruskin University
melanie.bell@anglia.ac.uk

Martin Schäfer
Friedrich-Schiller-Universität Jena
post@martinschaefer.info

Abstract

Using data from Reddy et al. (2011), we present a series of regression models of semantic transparency in compound nouns. The results indicate that the frequencies of the compound constituents, the semantic relation between the constituents, and metaphorical shift of a constituent or of the compound as a whole, all contribute to the overall perceived level of transparency. While not proposing an actual distributional model of transparency, we hypothesise that incorporating this information into such a model would improve its success and we suggest some ways this might be possible.

1 Introduction

Recently, a number of studies in distributional semantics have addressed the semantics of NN and AN compounds and phrases. Under the heading of compositionality, they often discuss phenomena that in the psycholinguistic and morphological literature are cast as issues of semantic transparency. In this paper, we are not proposing an actual distributional model of semantic transparency, but rather making some linguistic observations which have consequences for distributional models that attempt to capture the phenomenon. In Section 2, we introduce the notion of semantic transparency and its relation to compositionality in distributional semantics, and in Section 3 we present our descriptive framework for the semantics of complex nominals. Sections 4 and 5 describe the method and results, respectively, of our empirical study based on the data from Reddy et al. (2011), which we recode and use to build four regression models with semantic transparency as the dependent variable. Finally, Section 6 discusses the implications of our results for distributional models.

2 Semantic transparency and compositionality

The term 'semantic transparency' aims to capture the intuitive difference felt between compounds like *hogwash*, meaning 'nonsense', and a compound like *milkman*. In the literature, semantic transparency is defined in two main ways. One is the idea that it can be linked to meaning predictability. Plag (2003, 46) states that words are semantically transparent if "[...] their meaning is predictable on the basis of the word-formation rule according to which they have been formed." According to this definition, *hogwash* is clearly not transparent. But the meaning of *milkman* also does not seem predictable. Assuming the standard dictionary definition *man who delivers milk to people's houses*, are we to assume that there is a word formation rule of the kind *x who delivers y to people's houses*? This kind of definition seems excessively restrictive. The second kind of definition uses analysability rather than predictability. A classic example is Zwitserlood (1994, 344), who writes that "[t]he meaning of a fully transparent compound is synchronically related to the meaning of its composite words [...]". In this sense, *milkman* clearly is transparent because any possible usage will allow linking the interpretation in some way to the meanings of the constituent parts. But here the problem seems to be that the definition is too wide. Even in cases like *buttercup*, the name for the small flower with the yellow head, the meaning is related to the meanings of its composite words, because *butter* stands for the colour and *cup* for the shape of the actual flower.

While we know of no work that gives empirical correlates for establishing semantic transparency in terms of the meaning predictability approach, many psycholinguistic studies develop classification schemes that correspond to the second approach to transparency, e.g. Zwitserlood (1994), Libben et al. (2003). Besides psycholinguistics, the term semantic transparency also occurs in standard linguistic works on compounds, e.g. the discussion of anaphoric islands in Ward et al. (1991).

In lieu of the term semantic transparency, some psycholinguistic and linguistic studies use the term 'semantic compositionality' to refer to similar phenomena, and this tradition of using semantic compositionality also occurs in some studies within distributional semantics. In formal semantics, however, semantic compositionality is typically used to describe sentence-level semantic processes, namely, that the meaning of a complex expression is composed of the meanings of its constituent expressions and the rules used to combine them. However, if we accept underspecified semantic representations, then almost all meanings are compositional. For example, taking *milkman* again, if its meaning is composed by combining the two predicates MILK(x) and MAN(x) with the help of the underspecified template in (1), where R represents an underspecified relation, this is technically semantically fully compositional.

(1) λ B λ A λ y λ x [A(x) & R(x,y) & B(y)]

On this view, semantic transparency can still be seen as a compositionality issue in so far as it correlates with the amount of additional input that is involved in arriving at the meaning of a complex expression.

2.1 Compositionality in distributional approaches to XN semantics

Distributional studies of compositionality differ in what they actually try to model. Of most relevance here are composition models that try to model human judgements about XNs with the help of the vectors of their constituents and some compositionality function. Mitchell and Lapata (2010), for example, try to model human responses to a compound noun similarity task. Marelli et al. (2012) investigate the relation between distribution-based semantic transparency measures of compounds and constituent frequency effect in lexical decision latencies. Reddy et al. (2011) is a very good example where compositionality clearly corresponds to semantic transparency. While the term 'semantic transparency' does not occur in the paper, Reddy et al. (2011, 211) adapt the following definition of compound compositionality proposed in Bannard et al. (2003, 66): "[...] the overall semantics of the MWE [multi word expression] can be composed from the simplex semantics of its parts, as described (explicitly or implicitly) in a finite lexicon." This is reminiscent of Plag's definition of semantic transparency, and the link to semantic transparency becomes even clearer when looking at their operationalisation of the term. For the purposes of their paper, compositionality is equated with literality, and the aim of their models is to predict human ratings of compound literality. The compound literality ratings were elicited by asking the subjects to give a score ranging from 0 to 5 for how literal the phrase XY is, with a score of 5 indicating 'to be understood very literally', and a score of 0 indicating 'not to be understood literally at all'. Since we use their data for the models presented here, we will simply adopt their view and treat their literality ratings as compositionality or, in our terms, semantic transparency measures.

To model the literality ratings of their subjects, Reddy et al. (2011) used a vector space model of meaning and compared the performance of constituent based models and composition function based models. For the constituent based models, literality scores for the constituents were computed, where literality was defined as similarity between compound and constituent co-occurrence vectors. The compound literality was then calculated by using 5 different functions, including additive and multiplicative functions. In contrast, for the composition function based models, a vector for the compound was composed from the vectors of its constituents. The compositionality score was then measured by comparing the resulting compound score with the vector of the compound calculated from the corpus. All the models were then evaluated against the human judgments on the compound literality (the constituent based models also against the constituent literality judgements). Among the constituent based models, those that used an additive or a combinatorial function performed best, but not as good as the composition function based models. Reddy et al. (2011, 217) hypothesize that "[t]he reason could be because while constituent based models use contextual information of each constituent *independently*, composition function models make use of collective evidence from the contexts of both the constituents *simultaneously*."

3 A descriptive framework for semantic transparency

In order to capture and classify the internal semantic relations involved in semantic transparency, we start from the underspecified predicate logic notation in (2), which repeats (1), where A stands for the first part of a complex nominal, and B for the second part.

(2) $\lambda B \lambda A \lambda y \lambda x [A(x) \& R(x,y) \& B(y)]$

We assume that an underspecified relation R links the denotations of A and B in a given construction. Based on this, we developed the scheme given in figure 1, where, for reasons of perspicuity, we omitted the arguments of the predicates (note that in a full model, they are needed, because they can be shifted independently from the predicates).

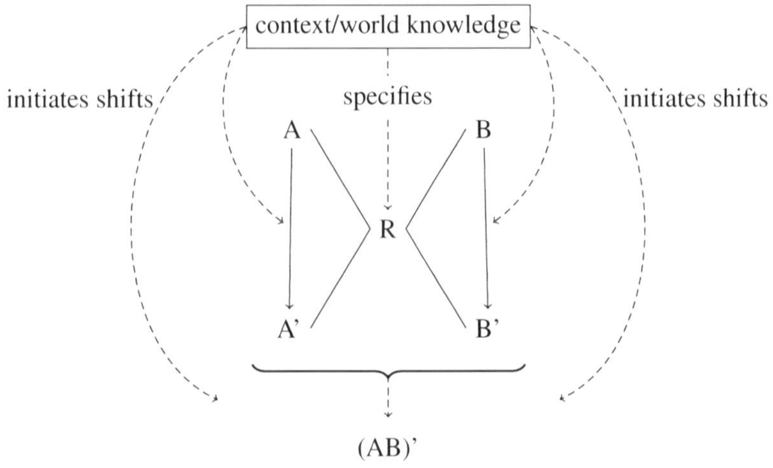

Figure 1: Scheme for A B combinatorics

As the scheme indicates, we assume that context and world knowledge are responsible for any further specification of the meaning of an AB combination. Specifically, we assume that A as well as B can be shifted from their literal meaning to a secondary meaning, labeled A' and B'. Metaphors and metonyms presents types of well-known shifts, other candidates would be e.g. the process of meaning differentiation, cf. Bierwisch (1982). However, even after a shift, they are still linked to the other part of the construction via the R relation. This kind of semantics for A B combinations therefore clearly falls into the category of radically underspecified approaches (cf. the characterization in Blutner (1998, 128)), and is much in the spirit of the ideas in Fanselow (1981) about the analysis of determinative compounds, and with him we assume that the specification of the exact relationship between the denotations as well as the shifts of the A and B parts fall into the domain of pragmatics.

The most basic configuration possible would be one where A and B retain their original meaning, and the relationship is set to identity. That is, the property expressed by A and by B hold of the very same entity, and the semantics is thus intersective. These combinations might be regarded as the most transparent AB combinations. Classic examples result from the combination of Kamp's (1975) predicative adjectives with a nominal head, e.g. *fourlegged animal*. However, even for standard examples of intersective modification further differentiation is needed, cf. the overview in Blutner (1998), and Kennedy (2007) specifically for gradable adjectives. We will give examples for shifted As and Bs in section 4.2.

The relation R As mentioned above, the underlying semantic format we assume is radically underspecified, and it is pragmatics and world knowledge that determine how the parameter R is specified. Since we hypothesize that the exact specification of R will have an influence on the semantic transparency of the AB combination, we need a way to distinguish between different possibilities of fixing R. Proposals for generalizations over this R relation can be taken from the large literature essentially concerned with developing generalizations over possible relations, for English most famously in Lees (1970), Warren (1978) and Levi (1978). We chose the classification scheme from Levi (1978) (cf. also the discussion in Ó Séaghdha (2008)), fully aware that her scheme, or in fact any generalized scheme, will not allow one to reproduce the exact meaning nor all the possible meanings of AB combinations (for comprehensive criticism to this end, cf. Downing (1977); Fanselow (1981)). On the other hand, note that Gagné and Spalding (2009), in a series of priming experiments, find that the ease of deriving the meaning of a compound word 'is mutually determined by the ease with which the constituents can be assigned to a particular role within a relational structure and by the availability of the appropriate relational structure.' Since there is evidence that these relational structures have psychological reality, it seems likely that not only the semantics of the individual constituents, but also the relation between them, contributes to overall level of transparency.

In our scheme, we also allow for whole compound shifts. At this point, we just indicate this possibility by the (AB)' in the scheme, without distinguishing in detail between the further internal possibilities. A very clear example of a whole compound shift is the derogative *asshole*, examples from the dataset used later include *ivory tower* and *cloud nine*. The complex possibilities can be illustrated by a combination like *buttercup*, discussed in the introduction.

4 Method

To test our hypothesis that the degree of semantic transparency of a complex nominal will be affected by the semantic relation between its constituents as well as shifts in meaning of the constituents or of the construction as a whole, we devised a series of regression models.

4.1 Dataset

We used the publicly available data set collected for and described in Reddy et al. (2011) (see the references for the download site). These authors selected a set of 90 compound nouns from the ukWaC corpus, a large web-derived corpus of English (Ferraresi et al. 2008). The sample was selected semi-randomly in such a way as to maximise the probability that it included different degrees of semantic transparency. Furthermore, all the selected compounds occurred at least 50 times in the corpus. For each of the 90 compounds, Reddy et al. obtained literality ratings from 30 raters. Importantly, the individual raters went through two distinct steps in rating each of the items. First, the rater was presented with 'all possible definitions' (Reddy et al. 2011) of the compound under investigation: in practice 1 or 2 definitions. The rater was asked to read through 5 randomly selected example sentences containing the compound and, for compounds with alternative definitions, decide which definition applied most frequently. In the second step, they were asked to rate either (a) how literal they perceived the compound to be, or (b) how literally the first constituent was used in the compound or (c) how literally the second constituent was used in the compound. This procedure has two important advantages: firstly, compounds are always presented in context, avoiding the artificiality associated with presenting words in isolation, and secondly, forcing the raters to settle on the most frequent definition ensures that the subsequent ratings are made for the compound with this particular reading. This elegantly avoids the usual problems that arise from the ubiquitous vagueness and ambiguity of compounds. For the purposes of this study we assume that the perceived literality of a compound or compound constituent is a measure of its semantic transparency.

The Reddy et al. dataset contains 30 ratings for each of the three tasks (a-c above) for all 90 compounds: in other words, a total of 8100 ratings. However, because tasks were assigned randomly to raters, the same rater did not necessarily perform all three tasks for any given compound. Since we wanted to use the perceived literality of the constituents to predict the perceived literality of the compound, we chose to use within-subject comparisons: this would allow us to model how well an individual's perception of constituent literality predicts their compound literality rating. From the total dataset, we therefore extracted only those items for which the same rater had performed all three tasks. This produced a set of 1337 tokens for which literality judgements for each constituent as well as the compound as a whole had been given by a single person. Within this set, 12 of the 90 compound types showed variation in the definition assigned, i.e. each of the possible definitions had been chosen by at least one rater. Because we were interested in the relationship between semantic structure and literality ratings, we wanted to code and analyse these different readings separately from one another. A token-based analysis allowed us to do this since, for each token, the dataset indicates the definition assigned by the rater in question.

4.2 Categories coded

We coded this set of compounds for a variety of semantic and frequency-based variables.[1] The semantic coding was definition-specific: each token was coded according to the definition chosen by the particular literality rater, so different tokens of the same compound did not necessarily receive identical coding. To encode the relations that can be used to specify the R-parameter, we used the classification system of Levi (1978) which has proven itself to be useful in computational linguistics (cf. Ó Séaghdha 2008). As far as shifts of the A and B constituents were concerned, we only distinguished between metaphorical and metonymic shifts. This coding was done by two linguists (the authors), one a trained semanticist and the other a native speaker of English: we first coded independently, and then discussed the results to reach a consensus about those items where we initially disagreed. For two compounds, *kangaroo court* and *flea market*, we were unable to reach consensus and these were therefore subsequently excluded.

The following examples from the dataset illustrate our coding scheme: *application form*, defined as *a form to use when making an application*, was classified as having unshifted first and second constituents, and the parameter R was set to FOR ('a form for an application'). In contrast, *crash course*, defined as *a rapid and intense course of training or research*, contains a metaphorical shift of the first element ('sth. fast and intense'), and R is set to BE. A metaphorical shift of the second element is exemplified by *eye candy*, where *candy* is shifted to mean *something pleasing but intellectually undemanding*. Again, the relationship is FOR. *Ground floor* exemplifies the IN-relation, which includes temporal and spatial location, and *brick wall* exemplifies the MAKE (TYPE 2) relation.

We also coded whether the compound as a whole had been shifted, as in *ivory tower* for example. *Ivory tower* as a whole stands for 'A condition of seclusion or separation from the world' (OED online), and it is not possible to synchronically decompose it further in any sensible way. However, it is clear to the native speaker that there has been a shift; otherwise it is unexplainable why, although neither *ivory* nor *tower* have anything to do with its current meaning, the concept of *tower* still shines through in expressions like *live in ivory towers/assault their ivory towers/geek atop an ivory tower*.

In addition, we extracted various frequency measures from the British National Corpus, namely the lemmatised frequencies of the individual constituents and of the whole compound written spaced and unspaced (either hyphenated or as a single word). On the basis of the last two of these measures, we calculated the 'spelling ratio' for each compound: this is the proportion of tokens that are written unspaced, which is taken to be a measure of the degree of lexicalization (Bell and Plag 2012).

4.3 Statistical analysis

The frequency and semantic variables were used as predictors in ordinary least squares regression analyses with literality of the compound or its constituents as the dependent variables. To alleviate the potentially harmful effects of extreme values on our statistical models, all quantitative predictors were first logarithmatised. Some of the semantic categories, including all metonymical shifts and several values of R, applied to very few compounds in the dataset. This would greatly reduce the power of any statistical analysis involving these variables: failure to reach significance could be simply the result of low frequency in this particular set of compounds or significant effects could be due to other features of those particular types. We therefore included in the analyses only metaphorical shifts and the three most frequent values of R, namely FOR, IN and BE. Each of the classes coded was represented by at least 9 types (i.e. compound senses) and 140 tokens in our data.

[1]Our semantic codings are available at www.martinschaefer.info/publications/TFDS-2013/TFDS-2013_Bell_Schaefer.zip

	Coef	S.E.	t	Pr(> $|z|$)
Intercept	-0.5861	0.3207	-1.83	0.0678
logFreqN1	0.2830	0.0243	11.63	<0.0001
logFreqN2	0.1535	0.0283	5.42	<0.0001
spellingRatio	-0.1240	0.0249	-4.98	<0.0001
Ametaphor=Yes	-0.6397	0.0939	-6.82	<0.0001
Bmetaphor=Yes	-0.4841	0.0920	-5.26	<0.0001
ABmetaphor=Yes	-1.8411	0.0910	-20.23	<0.0001
In=Yes	0.6041	0.1273	4.75	<0.0001
For=Yes	0.2363	0.0882	2.68	0.0074

Table 1: Final model for compound literality using semantic and frequency-based predictors, $R^2 = 0.459$

	Coef	S.E.	t	Pr(> $|z|$)
Intercept	-0.8117	0.2211	-3.67	0.0003
literality of A	0.4558	0.0179	25.43	<0.0001
literality of B	0.4147	0.0180	23.03	<0.0001
logFreqN1	0.0804	0.0179	4.50	<0.0001
logFreqN2	0.0506	0.0196	2.58	0.0100
Ametaphor=Yes	-0.2361	0.0720	-3.28	0.0011
Bmetaphor=Yes	-0.2059	0.0726	-2.84	0.0046
ABmetaphor=Yes	-0.1849	0.0752	-2.46	0.0141

Table 2: Final model for compound literality including constituent literality ratings, $R^2 = 0.739$

5 Results

Model 1 We first modelled the overall literality of the compound, as given by the human raters, using our semantic and frequency-based variables as predictors. Table1 shows the final model, from which all non-significant predictors have been removed step-wise, following standard procedures of model simplification. In all tables in this paper, positive coefficients indicate a tendency towards higher literality, i.e. transparency, while negative coefficients indicate a tendency towards lower literality, i.e. opacity.

It can be seen that both types of predictor, semantic and frequency-based, were found to be statistically significant. Literality increases with increasing frequency of either constituent and, as might be expected, falls as the proportion of unspaced tokens increases (i.e. as lexicalization increases). Literality rating is lower when either constituent, or the whole compound, is metaphorical. Most significantly, however, certain semantic relations (FOR and IN) are associated with greater literality. On the assumption that literality is a measure of semantic transparency, this is the first evidence that the relation between constituents, as well as the semantics of the constituents themselves, contributes to transparency.

Model 2 We next included the human ratings for constituent literality as predictors, alongside those used in the previous model. Reddy et al. (ibid.) show that there is a strong correlation between the average literality scores for the compounds and those for their constituents, so we expected that the constituent literality scores would be highly significant predictors in our model. Furthermore, on the assumption that the properties of a constituent contribute to its degree of transparency, we hypothesised that the constituent literality ratings would subsume our other constituent-based variables, namely frequency and semantic shift. We therefore expected that these variables would become less significant or even insignificant in the presence of constituent literality. On the other hand, we expected that the effects of semantic relations and whole-compound metaphorical shifts would remain significant, since they are properties of the whole compound, rather than either constituent.

The final model, from which all non-significant predictors have been eliminated, is shown in Table 2. As expected, the literality ratings of the constituents are highly significant predictors of overall literal-

	Coef	S.E.	t	Pr(> |z|)
Intercept	-0.3791	0.3418	-1.11	0.2676
logFreqN1	0.3406	0.0262	12.99	<0.0001
logFreqN2	0.0953	0.0305	3.13	0.0018
spellingRatio	-0.0674	0.0268	-2.51	0.0122
Ametaphor=Yes	-1.7234	0.1003	-17.19	<0.0001
Bmetaphor=Yes	0.8728	0.0987	8.85	<0.0001
ABmetaphor=Yes	-1.8728	0.0939	-19.95	<0.0001
In=Yes	0.9275	0.1344	6.90	<0.0001

Table 3: Final model for literality of constituent A, $R^2 = 0.499$

	Coef	S.E.	t	Pr(> |z|)
Intercept	1.2383	0.3448	3.59	0.0003
logFreqN1	0.1224	0.0259	4.73	<0.0001
logFreqN2	0.1443	0.0304	4.75	<0.0001
spellingRatio	-0.1563	0.0264	-5.93	<0.0001
Ametaphor=Yes	0.8382	0.1009	8.31	<0.0001
Bmetaphor=Yes	-1.6511	0.0989	-16.70	<0.0001
ABmetaphor=Yes	-2.0563	0.0978	-21.02	<0.0001
For=Yes	0.2241	0.0929	2.41	0.0160

Table 4: Final model for literality of constituent B, $R^2 = 0.498$

ity: in each case, the more literal the constituent, the more literal the compound. Surprisingly, however, the other constituent-based variables remain significant even in the presence of the constituent literality ratings: though the effects are much weakened, an increase in frequency of either A or B still leads to greater overall transparency, while metaphorical shift of either constituent leads to greater opacity. It might be argued that the strong effects in our models of metaphorical shifts are a result of the data collection method: asking subjects to rate literality may have led them actually to rate the presence or absence of metaphor. However, if this were all they rated, we would not expect the effects of metaphorical shift of A or B to survive in model 2 alongside the constituent literality ratings, since both types of predictor would be accounting for the same portion of the variance. An even more unexpected finding is that, once constituent literality ratings are included in the model, lexicalisation and semantic relations become insignificant as predictors of overall transparency. This suggests that these relations are correlated with the literality of the constituents, so that they account for the same portion of the overall variation.

Models 3 and 4 To test the hypothesis that the semantic relation between compound constituents influences the extent to which the constituents are perceived as having literal readings, we constructed two models with the literality ratings of A and B respectively as the dependent variables, and our semantic and frequency-based variables as the predictors.

Table 3 shows the final model for literality of constituent A, with non-significant predictors removed. It can be seen that one semantic relation, IN, is indeed associated with an increase in perceived literality, and constituent A is also perceived as more literal as the frequency of *either* constituent increases. On the other hand, when the compound is more highly lexicalized (as indicated by a higher spelling ratio), or when the whole compound has undergone metaphorical shift, constituent A is perceived as less literal; similarly, when A itself has shifted metaphorically, it is perceived as less literal. However, in contrast to the frequency effects, metaphorical shift of B leads to A being perceived as more literal, presumably relative to B. Table 4 shows the final model for literality of constituent B, again with non-significant predictors removed. This is very similar to the model for A except that here the relation FOR is associated with an increase in perceived literality.

It is interesting both that the effect of semantic relation on compound transparency is mediated through the transparency of the constituents, and that each constituent is associted with a different relation in this respect. The results tie in with recent work on prosodic prominence in the English NN. Plag et al. (2008), for example, demonstrate that the FOR relation is correlated with stress on N1, whereas IN is correlated with stress on N2. Furthermore Bell and Plag (2012) show that stress tends to fall on the most informative constituent. If FOR is associated with greater transparency of N2, that might explain why in such compounds stress tends to fall on N1, the assumption being that the less transparent constituent is also the more informative. The reverse pattern would hold in the case of compounds with R set to IN: N1 is more transparent, hence N2 is relatively more informative, hence prone to be stressed.

6 Consequences for distributional semantics

The findings described in this paper pose challenges for a distributional account of semantic transparency. In particular, if the aim is to use distributional semantics as a tool to understand human language processing, then those semantic factors that play a role in human processing should be reflected in distributional models. And, although the models of human literality ratings tested by Reddy et al. (2011) are not unsuccesful, there is still room for improvement. The strong effects of constituent frequency in our models, for example, suggest that it would be worth experimenting with different ways of introducing frequency-based weightings. We also hypothesise that taking into account the internal semantic structure of the data could further improve model performance. In this respect, we see two promising directions that can be explored, one concerning shifts, the other concerning semantic relations.

Vecchi et al. (2011) use distributional semantics to characterise semantic deviance in ANs. Unattested ANs were rated by two of the authors using a 3-point scale (deviant, intermediate or acceptable), where the two endpoints marked 'semantically highly anomalous, regardless of effort' vs. 'completely acceptable'. Only those items with inter-rater agreement on 'deviant' or 'acceptable' were included in the test set. They investigated the ability of three measures to distinguish between deviant and non-deviant ANs: length of the AN vectors, cosine similarity between vectors for AN and N, and the average cosine with the top 10 nearest neighbours (density). Of these three indices, only the first and the last yield significant results for AN classification. The authors hypothesize that a wide angle between N and AN might not be a measure of deviance, but rather a common feature of a number of types of non-deviant ANs, among them metaphorical constructions. If they are correct, it should be possible to use cosine similarity on acceptable AN combinations in order to identify shifts.

However, it is not clear to what extent the distinction between unattested metaphorical and deviant types is real. The examples given by Vecchi et al. (ibid.) suggest that the difference may be a matter of degree and related to semantic transparency. Combinations were rated as deviant if the authors found them 'semantically highly anomalous no matter how much effort one put in', but there was very low inter-rater agreement, and all four examples of deviant types given in the paper seem to us effortlessly interpretable: e.g. you might suffer with an *academic bladder* if you need to urinate every 50 minutes, *blind pronunciation* could be the attempted pronunciation of a word in a language you don't recognise, *sharp glue* could be glue with a pH less than 7 and, by analogy with *couch potato*, a *parliamentary potato* could be a parliamentarian who spends a lot of time on the benches but makes little contribution to the proceedings. However, all these interpretations, though readily available, involve semantic shifts and are therefore relatively opaque according to our model. Vecchi et al's (ibid.) acceptable examples, on the other hand, are relatively transparent. Three of these, *vulnerable gunman*, *huge joystick* and *blind cook* have obvious literal interpretations where there is no shift and R is set to identity, in addition to any possible metaphorical meanings. The fourth, *academic crusade* also has fairly obvious possible meanings involving a shift only of *crusade* (a crusade by academics, for example) and the shift of *crusade* from its original meaning is now so frequent that it is debatable whether it is a shift at all. Deciding at what point a diachronically shifted meaning becomes central was one of the difficulties we had when coding our data cf. *china* in *china clay* and *web* in *web site*. In a similar vein, a reviewer points out that one reason for the correlation between transparency and constituent frequency might be that shifted meanings are more likely to be taken as literal/lexicalised with more frequent words. Vecchi et al. (ibid.)

themselves acknowledge that 'semantically deviant' expressions might be interpretable metaphorically, and suggest that distributional measures might 'naturally lead to a gradient notion of semantic anomaly'. It seems that such a notion of semantic anomaly is in fact very close to our notion of semantic opacity, and it would therefore be very interesting to devise distributional models similar to those used by Vecchi et al. (ibid.) for the data collected by Reddy et al. (2011). If we are right that the two notions are similar and that a single model of transparency can encompass all complex nominals, then we would expect to find similar results.

With regard to semantic relations, the situation is a bit more challenging. A fairly straightforward first step might be to use a compound classification algorithm on the data.[2] Ideally, this should be combined with automatic selection of the relevant senses of the compound constituents using the methodology described in Reddy et al. (2011), i.e. by using either static or dynamic prototypes. Another relevant study is Boleda et al. (2012) who evaluate different composition functions with respect to their ability to model the distinction between three types of adjectival modifier: intersective, subsective, and intensional. These are exemplified in the AN combinations *white towel*, *white wine* and *former bassist* respectively. In terms of our model, the three types can be seen as representing a cline in transparency, with intersective types the most transparent and intensional types the most relatively opaque. Boleda et al. (ibid.) find that the cosine between the A and AN vectors differs significantly between the three groups, being highest for intersective types, lowest for intensional types and intermediate for subsective. There was little difference between the groups when A was compared with N, or AN was compared with N. Likewise, Reddy et al. (2011) obtained much better results for compound literality modelled on the basis of N1 alone, than on the basis of N2 alone. These results suggest that, in a distributional model of AB semantic transparency, the vector for A should be given more weighting than the vector for B. This might also partly explain why Vecchi et al. (2011) did not get significant results using the cosine between AN and N.

Acknowledgements

We thank the three anonymous reviewers for their advice and comments, and we especially thank Aurelie Herbelot for a most fruitful abundance of the same.

References

Bannard, C., T. Baldwin, and A. Lascarides (2003). A statistical approach to the semantics of verb-particles. In *Proceedings of the ACL 2003 workshop on Multiword expressions: analysis, acquisition and treatment - Volume 18*, MWE '03, Stroudsburg, PA, USA, pp. 65–72. Association for Computational Linguistics.

Bell, M. J. and I. Plag (2012). Informativeness is a determinant of compound stress in English. *Journal of Linguistics 48*(3), 485–520.

Bierwisch, M. (1982). Formal and lexical semantics. *Linguistische Berichte* (80), 3–17.

Blutner, R. (1998). Lexical pragmatics. *Journal of Semantics 15*(2), 115–162.

Boleda, G., E. M. Vecchi, M. Cornudella, and L. McNally (2012). First-order vs. higher-order modification in distributional semantics. In *Proceedings of the 2012 Joint Conference on Empirical Methods in Natural Language Processing and Computational Natural Language Learning*, Juju Island, Korea, pp. 1223–1233. Association for Computational Linguistics.

Downing, P. (1977). On the creation and use of english compound nouns. *Language 53*(4), 810–842.

Fanselow, G. (1981). *Zur Syntax und Semantik der Nominalkomposition*, Volume 107 of *Linguistische Arbeiten*. Tübingen: Niemeyer.

[2] This was suggested by Aurelie Herbelot.

Ferraresi, A., E. Zanchetta, M. Baroni, and S. Bernardini (2008). Introducing and evaluating ukwac, a very large web-derived corpus of english. In *Proceedings of the WAC4 Workshop at LREC 2008*, Marrakech. ELRA.

Gagné, C. L. and T. L. Spalding (2009). Constituent integration during the processing of compound words: Does it involve the use of relational structures? *Journal of Memory and Language 60*, 20–35.

Kamp, H. (1975). Two theories about adjectives. In E. L. Keenan (Ed.), *Formal Semantics for natural languages*, pp. 123–155. Cambridge, UK: Cambridge University Press.

Kennedy, C. (2007). Vagueness and grammar: The semantics of relative and absolute gradable adjectives. *Linguistics and Philosophy 30*, 1–45.

Lees, R. B. (1970). *The Grammar of English Nominalization.* The Hague: Mouton.

Levi, J. N. (1978). *The syntax and semantics of complex nominals.* New York: Academic Press.

Libben, G., M. Gibson, Y. B. Yoon, and D. Sandra (2003). Compound fracture: The role of semantic transparency and morphological headedness. *Brain and Language 84*, 50–64.

Marelli, M., G. Dinu, R. Zamparelli, and M. Baroni (2012). Semantic transparency and the distributional origin of constituent effects in compound processing. Poster presented at the conference Architectures and Mechanisms for Language Processing (AMLAP) 2012, Riva del Garda, Italy, September 6-8.

Mitchell, J. and M. Lapata (2010). Composition in distributional models of semantics. *Cognitive Science 34*(8), 1388–1429.

Ó Séaghdha, D. (2008). Learning compound noun semantics. Technical Report 735, Computer Laboratory, University of Cambridge.

Plag, I. (2003). *Word-Formation in English.* Cambridge: Cambridge University Press.

Plag, I., G. Kunter, S. Lappe, and M. Braun (2008). The role of semantics, argument structure, and lexicalization in compound stress assignment in english. *Language 84.4*, 760–794.

Reddy, S., I. P. Klapaftis, D. McCarthy, and S. Manandhar (2011, November). Dynamic and static prototype vectors for semantic composition. In *Proceedings of The 5th International Joint Conference on Natural Language Processing 2011 (IJCNLP 2011)*, Chiang Mai, Thailand.

Reddy, S., D. McCarthy, and S. Manandhar (2011). An empirical study on compositionality in compound nouns. In *Proceedings of the 5th International Conference on Natural Language Processing*, Chiang Mai, Thailand, pp. 210–218. AFNLP. All data for the paper is available from the following site: `http://sivareddy.in/papers/files/ijcnlp_compositionality_data.tgz`.

Vecchi, E. M., M. Baroni, and R. Zamparelli (2011). (linear) maps of the impossible: Capturing semantic anomalies in distributional space. In *Proceedings of the DISCO (Distributional Semantics and Compositionality) Workshop at ACL 2011*, East Stroudsburg PA, pp. 1–9. ACL.

Ward, G., R. Sproat, and G. McKoon (1991). A pragmatic analysis of so-called anaphoric islands. *Language 67*(3), 439–474.

Warren, B. (1978). *Semantic patterns of noun-noun compounds.* Number 41 in Gothenburg studies in English. Göteborg: Acta Universitatis Gothoburgensis.

Zwitserlood, P. (1994). The role of semantic transparency in the processing and representation of Dutch compounds. *Language and cognitive processes 9*(3), 341–368.

Can distributional approaches improve on Good Old-Fashioned Lexical Semantics?

Ann Copestake

Computer Laboratory, University of Cambridge
aac10@cl.cam.ac.uk

Abstract

In this position paper, I discuss some linguistic problems that computational work on lexical semantics has attempted to address in the past and the implications for alternative models which incorporate distributional information. I concentrate in particular on phenomena involving count/mass distinctions, where older approaches attempted to use lexical semantics in their models of syntax. I outline methods by which the earlier models allowed the transmission of information between lexical items (regular polysemy and inheritance) and address the possibility that similar techniques could usefully be incorporated into distributional models.

1 Introduction

While there has been much recent discussion of techniques for developing compositional approaches to distributional semantics, especially with respect to particular categories of phrase (e.g., adjective-noun), as far as I am aware, there has been no attempt to discuss systematically all the roles that distributional semantic representations might play in the production of a model of a sentence. Indeed, from the viewpoint of researchers working on 'traditional' areas of computational linguistics, such as parsing and generation, and those primarily interested in modeling language for its own sake, rather than application-building, the extensive work on distributional semantics has been somewhat disappointing in failing to provide models which are integrated with existing work to help solve long-standing problems. In some respects, most work on distributional semantics lacks ambition compared to earlier research on lexical semantics, in that previous approaches at least attempted to provide accounts that were fully integrated with syntax and full-coverage compositional semantics: i.e., which used lexical semantics as part of the models that assigned syntactic structure or logical form.[1] There are reasons to think that distributional approaches could well be more appropriate in such contexts, but a demonstration of this will involve looking at a broad range of phenomena. This paper is intended as a first step in outlining some of the issues that might be considered.

I first want to distinguish the discussion of lexical meaning here from the various approaches to deriving distributional meaning from sentences investigated by Clark and Pulman (2007), Baroni and Zamparelli (2010), Mitchell and Lapata (2010), Guevara (2011) and others which in turn relates to previous approaches to combining connectionist and symbolic approaches (e.g., Smolensky and Legendre, 2006). That line of work assumes that a syntactic representation (or perhaps a logical form) is available to guide the process of composition of distributions.[2] This work is mostly orthogonal to the issue I wish

[1]Note that use 'compositional semantics' in its predominant sense to mean an approach in the tradition of Montague grammar, construed broadly, but including a treatment of quantification.

[2]I note the possibility of working with logical forms, since, although it is usual to work with syntactic relationships when working on compositional distributional semantics, the assumption is that these relationships are semantically meaningful. It thus seems possible that the models would, in principle, perform better if they were built on the basis of a logical form of some type, in that this provides a level of abstraction with respect to (some) verb alternations, expletive subjects and so on. Logical forms generally reflect a 'deeper' analysis which incorporates semantics associated with constructions, such as compound

to discuss here, which is whether the lexical phenomena addressed by earlier approaches might be modelled distributionally and whether this has implications for the overall architecture: for instance, in those case where lexical semantics affects syntax, some mechanism is required in the overall architecture to make syntax sensitive to the lexical semantic representation. This is not to say that there are no points of contact. For instance, in the notion of cocomposition described in Pustejovsky's Generative Lexicon (GL) work (e.g., Pustejovsky, 1995) the composition function is determined both by functor and argument. This can be perhaps related to some of the more recent work on composition with distributional semantics, where individual words can be associated with different composition functions (as suggested by Washtell (2011)). But GL is an exception in treating composition as part of a theory of lexical semantics, and even GL makes rather conventional assumptions about compositional semantics in many respects. Hence discussion of this is not part of the current paper.

I will concentrate here on research on modelling the behaviour of individual words rather than work on the traditional relationships between words (or word senses) — hyponymy, synonymy, antonymy and meronymy. Though this is not the focus of the current discussion, I will briefly touch on the use of hyponymy relationships in modelling the semantics of individual lexemes in §4.

At this point, a nomenclature issue arises, since there is no good collective term for the non-distributional approaches. 'Non-distributional' is clunky. To talk about 'traditional' or 'classical' lexical semantics seems inappropriate given the the earliest distributional work (e.g., Harris, 1954) predates, for example, the feature-based approach of Fodor and Katz (1963) (the first computational work on distributions was underway at this point, although the first publication I am aware of is Harper (1965)). The term 'symbolic' is problematic, since distributional semantics is also symbolic. So, in the absence of a better alternative, I will use 'Good old-fashioned lexical semantics' (GOFLS) by analogy with Haugeland's 'Good old-fashioned AI' (GOFAI: Haugeland, 1985). Hence the question that forms the title of this paper: "Can distributional approaches improve on Good Old-Fashioned Lexical Semantics?".

Models using hand-crafted GOFLS were integrated into parsing in a range of approaches from the 1970s onwards. For example, Boguraev (1979) used semantic preferences expressed in terms of semantic primitives specified by Wilks (1975) for disambiguation with an augmented transition network (ATN) parser. More complex models were later investigated within feature structure formalisms, perhaps most extensively within Pustejovsky's Generative Lexicon (GL) framework (Pustejovsky, 1995). Such approaches combine syntax, compositional and lexical semantics within one model and thus lexical semantics can influence and constrain syntax. This type of approach had some success in the 1980s and early 1990s in limited domains, but failed to scale to broad-coverage NLP. However, the models were (and are) nevertheless of interest to linguists and to psycholinguists. Seen from the perspective of using computational modeling to formally investigate language, they have therefore been partially successful.

Nevertheless, I think it is plausible to claim that the failure of GOFLS approaches in a computational setting was not just due to lack of resources to build highly complex lexicons, but to underlying problems with models that do not cope well with the 'messiness' of the actual data. Verspoor's detailed corpus investigation of some of the 'classic' GL cocomposition phenomena (Verspoor, 1997) is a case in point: to allow for the data there with a GOFLS model would have required fine-grained distinctions to be drawn which were otherwise unmotivated. Since that was precisely the problem with previous approaches to lexical semantics that had partly motivated the development of GL (see Pustejovsky's discussion and criticism of sense enumeration, for example), there was reason to doubt the classic GL model on theoretical grounds. Distributional-style approaches have been successfully adopted as models in investigation of some of the 'classic' GL phenomena (e.g., Lapata and Lascarides, 2003). However, these models are partial in that the distributional techniques have been used in isolation, rather than as part of an integrated syntactic-logical-distributional model. Furthermore, the aim in most published work is to show the best performance on a particular test set, rather than to build models which demonstrate good performance on a broad range of phenomena, let alone build fully-integrated broad-coverage systems.[3]

nouns and NPs acting as temporal modifiers. These might be expected to be relevant to the choice of functions for combining distributions.

[3]Baroni and Lenci (2010) argue convincingly that researchers should look at the performance of a single distributional

It therefore seems worthwhile to revisit some of the roles that GOFLS played in the earlier work, to investigate whether distributional semantics is really a promising alternative and to look at the requirements for distributional models under these assumptions. The viewpoint here is a theoretical/formal one (rather than practically-oriented NLP): what role can distributional models play in accounts of lexical meaning that aim to be linguistically (and psycholinguistically) plausible? The current paper is very preliminary — it concentrates on issues relating to the interaction of syntax and lexical semantics with respect to the count/mass distinction, and on the treatment of regular polysemy.

I will draw a distinction between the use of distributional techniques for acquisition of lexical semantic information for a GOFLS approach and models which use distributions directly. For instance, some approaches to interpreting compound nouns use semantic primitives to represent the relationships between the elements in the compound (such as Levi's classes: BE, HAVE and so on (Levi, 1978)). If these classes form part of the representation for the utterance, or are used in other processing, then even if the classes are determined via distributions, the final model is non-distributional. In contrast, a genuinely distributional model would represent the relationships themselves as distributions. Of course, the status of the primitives is not always clear in particular experiments: they may be seen as a convenient way of categorizing classes of distributions, for instance for evaluation purposes. Without the integration of models into larger frameworks, such distinctions are naturally a little fuzzy.

One deliberate omission here is any discussion of disambiguation or selectional preferences. It seems very plausible that distributions might be used to improve a parse-ranking model, and it is surprising there has been so little published work in this area, since it would seem a very useful way of evaluating different distributional techniques. That is, I would expect a good distributional model to be able to capture the sort of information about semantics that is necessary to resolve some proportion of coordination and PP-attachment ambiguities, and to be a much more satisfactory way of doing this than the earlier semantic primitive approaches. However, disambiguation in principle requires open-ended models of concepts. That is, in order to disambiguate some utterances, detailed knowledge of the world is required (as has long been recognised e.g., Fodor and Katz (1963)). To take a specific example:

(1) Follow the path from the bend in the road to the car park.

It is reasonable that distributional semantics might allow partial disambiguation of the PP-attachment (e.g., determining that 'in the road' attaches to 'bend'), but without context (which might only be apparent on the ground rather than in the text) it is not clear how to attach 'to the car park'. Indeed, examples of this type often cannot be disambiguated by human annotators who lack access to the full context. For this reason, we cannot use disambiguation examples to test what information needs to be accessible in principle in a particular model, since in the worst case any information could be relevant (i.e., disambiguation is AI-complete).

In this paper, I will use two interrelated phenomena in order to look at how distributional semantics might replace GOFLS and what sort of models might be required. In §2, I will discuss some semantic constraints on grammatical behaviour. A variety of phenomena related to regular polysemy are then discussed in §3.

2 Distributional semantics and syntactic distinctions

There are a number of roles that lexical semantics could/should play in a grammar. Perhaps the most fundamental is to ensure that constraints on syntactic behaviour that relate to semantic categories can be represented and that constraints on the relationship between syntactic behaviour and meaning can be captured.

For example, in English, uses of nouns which denote humans in an utterance may not be mass terms.[4] For example, (2) and (3) are ungrammatical because human-denoting nouns may not take *much*

model in a very broad range of contexts, but few published papers do this.

[4]This is an oversimplification. A full statement requires discussion of some of the complications of the mass/count distinction. For instance, there are nouns such as *troops* and *police* which are not classical count nouns because they have idiosyncratic

as a determiner.

(2) * Much children hate cabbage.

(3) * Much crowd was on the street.

An account of this generalization in a GOFLS framework might, for instance, state that lexical entries for all human-denoting noun lexemes inherit from a single general class, which has the desired syntactic properties associated with it. Numerous ways of implementing such generalizations have been developed, some incorporating defaults in the formalism so that exceptions could be allowed for. In any such approach, it is important that the semantic class can be justified and that multiple properties are predicted. For instance, the human-denoting nouns could also be predicted to occur with the relative pronoun *who* rather than *which*.

This assumes a lexicalist view of syntax. Some linguists (e.g., Borer, 2005) have argued that lexical entries do not specify detailed subcategorization information, mass/count distinctions and so on. The fact that grammaticality judgments involving subcategorization are graded rather than absolute can be taken to support such a view. Borer's approach is unimplemented (with the exception of Haugereid (2009)) but her viewpoint can, in fact, be seen as consistent with the way that Penn TreeBank derived grammars behave, in not ruling out utterances such as (2) or (3) or examples which violate subcategorization constraints (e.g., (4)).

(4) * I enjoy to run.

Indeed, even the broad coverage English Resource Grammar (ERG, Flickinger, 2000), which adopts an approach to syntax based on HPSG, and has a detailed lexicalist account of subcategorization which blocks examples such as (4), leaves most nouns as underspecified for count / mass distinctions, because so many nouns can appear in either mass or count contexts.

In a lexicalist account, if a lexeme like *lawyer* is marked as count, an utterance such as (5) is typically treated as ungrammatical (or extra-grammatical).

(5) In our legal method there is too much lawyer and too little law. [G. K. Chesterton]

It could only be interpreted by creating an extended (mass, non-human) use of *lawyer* (e.g., via lexical rule, in the manner discussed in the next section).[5] In a construction-based account, such as Borer's, this use of *lawyer* simply ends up as being marked as mass. In and of itself, this does not indicate that the sentence is in any way odd, or that the meaning differs from the count use of *lawyer*. A GOFLS account could perhaps be combined with a construction-based approach to enforce the constraint on human-denoting terms in a way which would result in *lawyer* being marked as non-human-denoting in (5), though, as far as I am aware, such an account has not been proposed in detail, let alone implemented.

The theoretical disadvantage of GOFLS combined with a lexicalist approach is that it requires additional mechanisms to account for examples such as (5) and constraining such mechanisms is difficult. The approach is often criticized as being over-stipulative. In contrast, the disadvantage of GOFLS combined with the constructional account would be that there is no indication that examples such as (5) are in any way odd or rare. Conversely, there is the problem that mass readings are available in contexts which are underspecified for mass/count, such as (6).

(6) The lawyer came into the room.

---

behaviour with numerals.

[5]Example 5 could be taken to be metalinguistic, but it is reasonably representative of the sort of examples cited in the linguistics literature to show that all lexemes have both count and mass uses. In (5), I would take *lawyer* to refer to a property rather than being human-denoting (in the sense of referring to an individual or groups of individuals). In very general terms, this meaning shift is predictable, in that it is one of a range of possible types of use of predominantly count nouns in a mass context, but it is not the sort of use that would be listed by a lexicographer, for instance. So at least in that respect, it is distinct from the cases of regular polysemy, discussed in §3.

Intuitively, at least, this seems wrong: mass uses of predominantly count nouns should only be available in marked contexts.

We can sketch an alternative distributional account which begins to address such problems. For current purposes, I will just describe how a distributional approach might be integrated with a construction-based grammar. The first thing to note is that any such account requires partitioning or clustering the distributional space for the nouns. The constraint that a human-denoting term cannot be mass is assumed to apply to uses, rather than to words/lexemes.[6] Nouns such as *lawyer* will be overwhelmingly count rather than mass, but the construction account allows for possibilities such as (5). For the time being, let's assume that the non-count/property use of *lawyer* is attested in the contexts from which the distributional model has been constructed (a possibly implausible assumption which I will return to below in §3). Of course the usual count use of *lawyer* will be much more frequent. If the contexts for *lawyer* include the determiners associated with it, the use of *much* will (hypothetically) only occur with a small numbers of uses. If the space of uses is partitioned or clustered into human-denoting vs property-denoting, contexts with *much* should only occur with the property uses. The boundary between human-denoting and non-human-denoting uses will be fuzzy, of course.

For the correlation with syntax to work, it must also be possible to partition the space of uses according to the count/mass behaviour. Clearly, whether a noun occurs with *much* would be directly accessible from a conventional distribution (if determiners were included), but other reflexes of count/mass behaviour require an extended notion of distribution, allowing sensitivity to morphological marking or plurality. It would be inappropriate to go into a detailed discussion of syntax here, so I will assume for simplicity that the count/mass distinction is binary, that all instances of a noun in an utterance can be marked as count, mass or underspecified, and that contexts contain such information. If the constraint that human-denoting noun uses are never mass terms is valid, then we would expect the human-denoting space in a distribution to only contain uses marked as count or underspecified. The generalization that human-denoting terms are never mass could (at least potentially) arise from distributions of the relevant nouns rather than being stipulated.

The only piece of work which I am aware of which looks at count-mass distinctions using distributions is Katz and Zamparelli (2011).[7] The paper demonstrates an initial result, which suggests that nouns which show large differences in semantics between singular and plural forms as measured using distributional techniques are predominantly mass (in that they are frequently found in contexts which select for mass terms, and infrequently found in contexts that select for count terms). This would fit with the assumption that some sort of meaning shift has to occur for a mass noun to be pluralized. However, the use of distributions here is limited to measuring semantic (dis)similarity. Building more complex models would require a corpus which makes distinctions between count and mass contexts systematically. The ERG-parsed Wikiwoods corpus (Flickinger et al., 2010) contains such information, but it is unclear whether this is sufficiently accurate to allow the relevant meaning shifts to be detected.

So this outline suggests something about the types of models that are of interest. Distributions must be sensitive to distinctions such as count / mass. If we take this as a syntactic distinction, then the appropriate models are ones in which distributions contain syntactic information.[8] The advantage of the distributional model over the GOFLS approaches is that frequency effects are an integral part, and hence there is a natural account of the oddness of examples such as (5). The problem, from a practical perspective, is that distributions created over individual instances produce a severe sparse data problem (cf Rapp, 2004).

It is also, of course, implausible to assume that unusual cases such as that illustrated in (5) will actually be attested for all lexemes where they are possible in principle. What is actually required is an approach where certain uses may be postulated even though not actually attested with a particular word. Rather than discuss this with respect to marginal examples such as (5), I will turn to the phenomenon of

[6]Of course, the distributions for mass and count versions of a lexeme could just be constructed separately, but this is analogous to the simplistic lexicalist account where there are multiple, unrelated, word senses.

[7]I am grateful to an anonymous reviewer for drawing my attention to this paper.

[8]Though, in fact, there are arguments in favour of treating count / mass as part of compositional semantics, for instance by having sorts on variables which distinguish between divisible and indivisible.

regular polysemy.

3 Regular polysemy

The term regular polysemy is used to refer to the phenomenon that word senses (or usages) are often related to one another and that similar patterns of senses are found in groups of words. For instance, in most cases the same word is used for animals and their meat, (e.g., *lamb*, *turkey*, *haddock*, but not *deer/venison*) with the animal use being count and the meat use mass. This can be seen as a sub-case of a general pattern of count-mass conversions, which has been generically referred to as 'grinding'. Regular polysemy has been extensively investigated in GOFLS. The empirical motivation for these accounts came from lexicography, and some of the computational implementations made use of information extracted from machine readable versions of conventional dictionaries (MRDs).

In an utterance such as:

(7) I've never seen so much turkey.

turkey is taken to be non-count. The role of lexical semantics is to ensure that this is associated with the correct meaning of the term (i.e., the meat rather than the animal sense). It should also ensure that a similar correlation can be made even in the case where the mass usage is previously unseen. For instance, speakers can understand a use of *crocodile* as in (8) and also generate it in an appropriate context, even if *crocodile* has not been seen as a mass term previously.

(8) I've never seen so much crocodile.

In a lexicalist account which associates mass/count with lexical entries, a new lexical entry for *crocodile* can be generated via a lexical rule, if *crocodile* is known to be of the appropriate type (e.g., 'animal'). See, for instance, Figure 1, taken from Copestake and Briscoe (1995). The full details of the rule encoding are irrelevant here, but the following points should be noted. '1' indicates the specification of the input to the lexical rule (the count term) and '0' the output. The boxed integers indicate information sharing, so, for instance, the rule does not affect spelling ('ORTH') because the input and output share the same value. GL 'qualia structure' is used to represent aspects of lexical semantics. The compositional semantic representation is to be interpreted as producing a new predicate from the input (e.g., if the input semantics were equivalent to $\lambda x[\text{rabbit}(x)]$ the output would be $\lambda x[\text{grinding(rabbit)}(x)]$). The syntactic effects come from the overall type of the structure (**lex-count-noun** and **lex-uncount-noun**). Lexical rules of this type can also be used for derivational morphology, which is relevant because some derivations show semantic relationships very similar or even identical to regular polysemy patterns.

An alternative approach (e.g., in Pustejovsky, 1995) involves combining the different senses/usages in a single structure via 'dot objects' (e.g., ANIMAL • MEAT). The assumption is that there are some regularities in the combination of types which are possible. Some contexts will select the ANIMAL use of a lexical item, while others will select the MEAT use. The dot object approach allows the ambiguity between the uses to be retained in some utterances, unlike the lexical rule account, but it is unclear whether this actually agrees with the linguistic and psycholinguistic evidence for this class of examples.

There are a number of criticisms that have been leveled at these different accounts, which I will not attempt to summarize here. Both, however, allow for regular polysemy as a fact about language which is to some extent conventional, rather than a fact about the world. This is much clearer with regular polysemy than with the marginal examples such as (5), since different languages show different polysemy patterns, and meaning shifts corresponding to regular polysemy in one language may be marked syntactically or by derivational morphology in others.

Regular polysemy has not been investigated much within distributional semantics (although see Boleda et al., 2012). Again, if there is a syntactic reflex, it is necessary to have a model which integrates this with the distributions to fully capture the effects. However, the point I want to discuss here is whether patterns in distributions can be used to predict semantic spaces which are too rare to be seen in the distributions of some lexemes. I take it that this reflects the situation which a human is in who

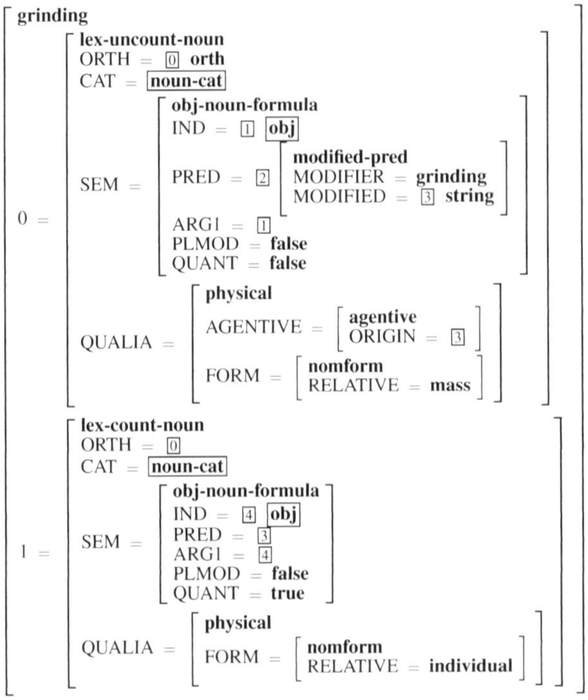

Figure 1: Grinding lexical rule from Copestake and Briscoe (1995)

hears an example such as (8) having never heard *crocodile* used as a mass term before. Schematically, we can imagine that the semantic spaces for words are as shown in Figure 2, where the unfilled circle by *crocodile* is supposed to indicate that this is a use that could be predicted based on the polysemy observed for other words, even though that use has not been observed by that particular hearer.

The theoretical attraction of such an account is that it incorporates frequency effects. It is neutral as to whether the different usages are to be taken as different senses: what it requires is just that the space of usages be partitionable. Whether novel uses could actually be predicted in this way is an empirical question, of course.

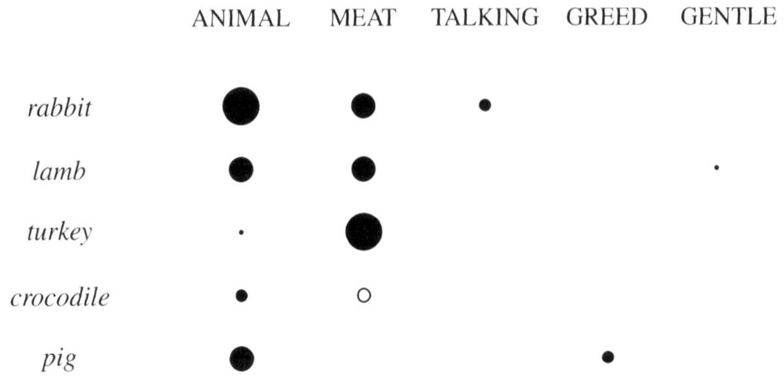

Figure 2: Schematic description of regular polysemy in terms of distributional spaces

4 Inheritance structure

A notable distinction between GOFLS accounts and distributional approaches is that most GOFLS approaches rely more-or-less heavily on some form of hierarchical structuring. In computational accounts, this can be used to allow inheritance or default inheritance. For instance, the GL qualia structure associated with the lexeme *book* might be inherited by *novel*. This allows semi-automatic construction of lexical entries with detailed lexical semantic information: for instance, in some earlier work taxonomies derived from MRDs were used to provide inheritance hierarchies and information about roles manually stipulated for the upper nodes only.

There is, of course, extensive computational work on deriving ontological relationships from corpora which is distributional in a broad use of the term, and also work on deriving such relationships from distributions in the narrower sense (e.g., Baroni et al., 2008). However, distributional models do not make use of inheritance relationships between words. Contexts which express hyponymy relationships, such as (9), will result in distributions for the hyponym which contain the hypernym (and vice versa), but that dimension is not distinguished in any way in the standard distributional approaches.

(9) Geese are waterfowl belonging to the tribe Anserini of the family Anatidae.

One way of thinking about the role of inheritance in GOFLS models is as a way of supplementing information about individual lexical items. For instance, if information about the qualia structure of a particular lexeme cannot be directly acquired, it might be obtained via inheritance. In an analogous manner, there seems to be scope for using automatically acquired ontological information in conjunction with distributional models, in particular to enrich the models of less frequent words. Distributional models require a considerable number of instances of words for good performance (and thus rely on the use of corpora which are vastly greater in size than anything which could plausibly correspond to the experience of an individual language learner). Ontology extraction systems, in contrast, achieve good performance on extraction of IS-A relationships with a single instance, provided the context for that instance is definitional in nature (dictionary definitions, Wikipedia articles and so on). It would thus seem natural to attempt to combine the two.

5 Conclusions

What I hope to have illustrated in this paper is that, to replace GOFLS accounts, distributional approaches will have to interact with syntax in a more integrated way than they currently do. That is, it is not enough to assume that distributions are created from syntactically parsed corpora and that distributions are composed in a manner guided by syntax, but that additionally syntax would have to be affected by distributions. I have tried to discuss ways in which distributional models could improve on GOFLS, and to suggest that they could, in fact, form part of the solution to some current linguistic debates.

The fact that distributional models are derived automatically from corpora is obviously a very strong point in their favour. But GOFLS models constructed from MRDs had an empirical basis too, and indeed, with the more modern dictionaries, the data was to some extent derived from corpora, albeit mediated by lexicographers. While there are obviously practical reasons to try and acquire all data directly from corpora, and while this makes the approaches more psycholinguisticall plausible (if plausible corpora are used), there may nevertheless be ways in which more definitional information could and should also be incorporated. For instance, I have suggested above that there may be a role for models which use corpus-derived ontological relationships to supplement the usual derivational models.

The topics I have outlined here are just a small selection of those which could have been discussed: taken as a whole I believe the comparison with prior work suggests the need for some more ambitious theoretical work on distributional approaches that takes into account more of the linguistic issues that have driven past work on lexical semantics.

Acknowledgements

This paper arises out of joint work with Aurélie Herbelot (currently unpublished, but available from `http://www.cl.cam.ac.uk/~aac10/papers/lc-current.pdf`). I am grateful to her and to the anonymous reviewers for comments. All errors (of commission and omission) are my own.

References

Baroni, M., S. Evert, and A. Lenci (2008). ESSLLI 2008 workshop on distributional lexical semantics.

Baroni, M. and A. Lenci (2010). Distributional memory: A general framework for corpus-based semantics. *Computational Linguistics 36*(4), 673–721.

Baroni, M. and R. Zamparelli (2010). Nouns are vectors, adjectives are matrices: Representing adjective-noun constructions in semantic space. In *Proceedings of the 2010 Conference on Empirical Methods in Natural Language Processing (EMNLP10)*, pp. 1183–1193.

Boguraev, B. (1979). *Automatic resolution of linguistic ambiguities.* Ph. D. thesis, University of Cambridge.

Boleda, G., S. Padó, and J. Utt (2012). Regular polysemy: A distributional model. In *Proceedings of *SEM*, pp. 151–160.

Borer, H. (2005). *Structuring Sense.* Oxford University Press.

Clark, S. and S. Pulman (2007). Combining Symbolic and Distributional Models of Meaning. In *Proceedings of the AAAI Spring Symposium on Quantum Interaction*, Stanford, CA, pp. 52–55.

Copestake, A. and T. Briscoe (1995). Semi-productive polysemy and sense extension. *Journal of Semantics 12:1*, 15–67.

Flickinger, D. (2000). On building a more efficient grammar by exploiting types. *Natural Language Engineering 6*(1), 15–28.

Flickinger, D., S. Oepen, and G. Ytrestøl (2010). Wikiwoods: Syntacto-semantic annotation for english wikipedia. In *Proceedings of the 7th International Conference on Language Resources and Evaluation*, pp. 1665–1671.

Fodor, J. and J. Katz (1963). The structure of a semantic theory. *Language 39*(2), 170–210.

Guevara, E. (2011). Computing semantic compositionality in distributional semantics. In *Proceedings of the Ninth International Conference on Computational Semantics (IWCS 2011)*, Oxford, England, UK, pp. 135–144.

Harper, K. E. (1965). Measurement of similarity between nouns. In *Proceedings of the 1st International Conference on Computational Linguistics (COLING65)*, New York, NY, pp. 1–23.

Harris, Z. (1954). Distributional Structure. *Word 10*(2-3), 146–162.

Haugeland, J. (1985). *Artificial Intelligence: The Very Idea.* MIT Press.

Haugereid, P. (2009). *A constructionalist grammar design, exemplified with Norwegian and English.* Ph. D. thesis, NTNU, Norwegian University of Science and Technology.

Katz, G. and R. Zamparelli (2011). Quantifying count/mass elasticity. In *Proceedings of 29th West Coast Conference on Formal Linguistics.*

Lapata, M. and A. Lascarides (2003). A Probabilistic Account of Logical Metonymy. *Computational Linguistics 29*(2), 261–315.

Levi, J. (1978). *The syntax and semantics of complex nominals.* Academic Press New York.

Mitchell, J. and M. Lapata (2010). Composition in Distributional Models of Semantics. *Cognitive Science 34*(8), 1388–1429.

Pustejovsky, J. (1995). *The Generative Lexicon.* MIT Press.

Rapp, R. (2004). A practical solution to the problem of automatic word sense induction. In *Proceedings of the ACL 2004 on Interactive poster and demonstration sessions*, pp. 26. Association for Computational Linguistics.

Smolensky, P. and G. Legendre (2006). *The Harmonic Mind.* MIT Press Cambridge, MA.

Verspoor, C. (1997). *Contextually-dependent lexical semantics.* Ph. D. thesis, University of Edinburgh. School of Informatics.

Washtell, J. (2011). Compositional expectation: A purely distributional model of compositional semantics. In *Proceedings of the Ninth International Conference on Computational Semantics (IWCS 2011)*, pp. 285–294.

Wilks, Y. (1975). A preferential, pattern-seeking, semantics for natural language inference. *Artificial Intelligence 6*(1), 53–74.

Sentence paraphrase detection: When determiners and word order make the difference

Nghia Pham
University of Trento
thenghia.pham@unitn.it

Raffaella Bernardi
University of Trento
bernardi@disi.unitn.it

Yao Zhong Zhang
The University of Tokyo
zhangyaoz@gmail.com

Marco Baroni
University of Trento
marco.baroni@unitn.it

Abstract

Researchers working on distributional semantics have recently taken up the challenge of going beyond lexical meaning and tackle the issue of compositionality. Several Compositional Distributional Semantics Models (CDSMs) have been developed and promising results have been obtained in evaluations carried out against data sets of small phrases and as well as data sets of sentences. However, we believe there is the need to further develop good evaluation tasks that show whether CDSM truly capture compositionality. To this end, we present an evaluation task that highlights some differences among the CDSMs currently available by challenging them in detecting semantic differences caused by word order switch and by determiner replacements. We take as starting point simple intransitive and transitive sentences describing similar events, that we consider to be paraphrases of each other but not of the foil paraphrases we generate from them. Only the models sensitive to word order and determiner phrase meaning and their role in the sentence composition will not be captured into the foils' trap.

1 Introduction

Distributional semantics models (DSMs) have recently taken the challenge to move up from lexical to compositional semantics. Through many years of almost exclusive focus on lexical semantics, many data sets have been developed to properly evaluate which aspects of lexical meaning and lexical relations are captured by DSMs. For instance, DSMs have been shown to obtain high performance in simulating semantic priming (Lund and Burgess, 1996), predicting semantic similarity (McDonald, 2000) and association (Griffiths et al., 2007) and have been shown to achieve human level performance on synonymy tests such as those included in the Test of English as a Foreign Language (TOEFL) (Landauer and Dumais, 1997). Compositional DSMs (CDSMs) are of more recent birth, and thus their proponents have focused effort on the study of the compositional operations that are mathematically available and empirically justifiable in vector-space models. Important progress has been made and several models have now been implemented ranging from the additive and multiplicative models of Mitchell and Lapata (2010), to functional models based on tensor contraction (Clark, 2012; Coecke et al., 2010; Baroni and Zamparelli, 2010), to the one based on recursive neural networks of Socher et al. (2011). We believe it is now necessary to shift focus somewhat to the semantic tasks against which to evaluate these models, and to develop appropriate data sets to better understand which aspects of natural language compositionality we are already capturing, what could still be achieved and what might be beyond the scope of this framework. This paper tries to contribute to this new effort. To this end, we start by looking at data sets of phrases and sentences used so far to evaluate CDSMs.

Word order in phrase similarity Starting from a data set of pairs of noun-noun, verb-noun and adjective-noun phrases (e.g., *certain circumstance* and *particular case*) rated by humans with respect to similarity (Mitchell and Lapata, 2010), Turney (2012) obtains an extended version including word order variations of the original phrases, which are automatically judged to have a very low similarity (e.g., *certain circumstance* and *case particular*).

Sentence similarity: Intransitive Sentences One of the first proposals to look at verb-argument composition traces back to Kintsch (2001) who was interested in capturing the different verb senses activated by different arguments, e.g., "*The color ran*" vs. "*The horse ran*", but the model was tested only on a few sentences. Starting from this work, Mitchell and Lapata (2008) made an important step forward by developing a larger data set of subject+intransitive-verb sentences. They began with frequent noun-verb tuples (e.g., *horse ran*) extracted from the British National Corpus (BNC) and paired them with sentences with two synonyms of the verb, representing distinct verb senses, one compatible and the other incompatible with the argument (e.g., *horse galloped* and *horse dissolved*). The tuples were converted into simple sentences (in past tense form) and articles were added to nouns when appropriate. The final data set consists of 120 sentences with 15 original verbs each composed with two subject nouns and paired with two synonyms. Sentence pair similarity was rated by 49 volunteers on the web.

Sentence similarity: Transitive Sentences Following the method proposed in Mitchell and Lapata (2008), Grefenstette and Sadrzadeh (2011b) developed an analogous data set of transitive sentences. Again the focus is on how arguments (subjects and objects) influence the selection of the meaning of an ambiguous verb. For instance, *meet* is synonymous both of *satisfy* and *visit*. For each verb (in total 10 verbs), 10 subject+transitive-verb+object tuples with the given verb were extracted from the BNC and sentences in simple past form (with articles if necessary) were generated. For example, starting from *met*, the two sentences "*The system met the criterion*" and "*The child met the house*" were generated. For each sentence, two new versions were created by replacing the verb with two synonyms representing two verb senses (e.g., "*The system visited the criterion*" and "*The system satisfied the criterion*"). The data set consists of 200 pairs of sentences annotated with human similarity judgments.

Large-scale full sentence paraphrasing data Socher et al. (2011) and Blacoe and Lapata (2012) tackle the challenging task of evaluating CDSMs against large-scale full sentence data. They use the Microsoft Research Paraphrase Corpus (Dolan et al., 2004) as data set. The corpus consists of 5800 pairs of sentences extracted from news sources on the web, along with human annotations indicating whether each pair captures a paraphrase/semantic equivalence relationship.

The evaluation experiments conducted against these data sets seem to support the following conclusions:

- "the model should be sensitive to the order of the words in a phrase (for composition) or a word pair (for relations), when the order affects the meaning." (Turney, 2012)
- "experimental results demonstrate that the multiplicative models are superior to the additive alternatives when compared against human judgments [about sentence similarity]." (Mitchell and Lapata, 2008)
- "shallow approaches are as good as more computationally intensive alternatives [in sentence paraphrase detection]. They achieve considerable semantic expressivity without any learning, sophisticated linguistic processing, or access to very large corpora." (Blacoe and Lapata, 2012)

With this paper, we want to put these conclusions on stand-by by asking the question of whether the appropriate tasks have really been tackled. The first conclusion above regarding word order is largely shared, but still no evaluation of CDSMs against sentence similarity considers word order seriously. We do not exclude that in real-world tasks systems which ignore word order may still attain satisfactory results (as the results of Blacoe and Lapata 2012 suggest), but this will not be evidence of having truly captured compositionality.

Moreover, a hidden conclusion (or, better, assumption!) of the evaluations conducted so far on CDSMs seems to be that grammatical words, in particular determiners, play no role in sentence meaning and hence sentence similarity and paraphrase detection. A first study on this class of words has been presented in Baroni et al. (2012) where it is shown that DSMs can indeed capture determiner meaning and their role in the entailment between quantifier phrases. The data sets used in Mitchell and Lapata (2008) and Grefenstette and Sadrzadeh (2011b) focus on verb meaning and its sense disambiguation within context, and consider sentences where determiners are just place-holders to simply guarantee grammaticality, but do not play any role neither in the human judgments nor in the model evaluation – in which they are simply ignored. Similarly, Blacoe and Lapata (2012) evaluate the compositional models on full sentences but again ignore the role of grammatical words that are treated as "stop-words". Should we conclude that from a distributional semantic view "*The system met the criterion*", "*No system met the criterion*" and "*Neither system met the criterion*" boil down to the same meaning? This is a conclusion we cannot exclude but neither accept *a-priori*. To start considering these questions more seriously, we built a data set of intransitive and transitive sentences in which word order and determiners have the chance to prove their worth in sentence similarity and paraphrase detection.

2 Compositional Distributional Semantic Models

In this section we won't present a proper overview of CDSMs, but focus only on those models we will be testing in our experiments, namely the multiplicative and additive models of Mitchell and Lapata (2008, 2009, 2010), and the lexical function model that represents the work carried out by Baroni and Zamparelli (2010), Grefenstette and Sadrzadeh (2011b), Grefenstette et al. (2013). We leave a re-implementation of Socher et al. (2012), another approach holding much promise for distributional composition with grammatical words, to future work.

Multiplicative and additive models While Mitchell and Lapata (2008, 2009, 2010) propose a general framework that encompasses most of the CDSMs currently available, their empirical work focuses on two simple but effective models where the components of the vector resulting from the composition of two input vectors contain (functions of) geometric or additive averages of the corresponding input components.

Given input vectors $\mathbf{u}$ and $\mathbf{v}$, the multiplicative model (`mult`) returns a composed vector $\mathbf{p}$ such that each of its components p_i is given by the product of the corresponding input components:

$$p_i = u_i v_i$$

In the additive model (`add`), the composed vector is a sum of the two input vectors:[1]

$$\mathbf{p} = \mathbf{u} + \mathbf{v}$$

Mitchell and Lapata do not address composition with grammatical words directly, but their approach is obviously aimed at capturing composition between content words.

Lexical function model Baroni and Zamparelli (2010) take inspiration from formal semantics to characterize composition in terms of *function application*. They model adjective-noun phrases by treating the adjective as a function from nouns onto (modified) nouns. Given that linear functions can be expressed by matrices and their application by matrix-by-vector multiplication, a functor (such as the adjective) is represented by a matrix $\mathbf{U}$ to be composed with the argument vector $\mathbf{v}$ (e.g., the noun vector) by multiplication, to return the vector representing the phrase:

$$\mathbf{p} = \mathbf{U}\mathbf{v}$$

[1]Mitchell and Lapata also propose two weighted additive models, but it is not clear how to extend them to composition of more than two words.

Non-terminals (Grammar)	Terminals (Lexicon)
$S \to DP\ VP$	$DET \to$ a; some; the; one; two; three; no
$DP \to DET\ N$	$N \to$ man; lady; violin; guitar; ...
$DP \to N$	$ADJ \to$ big; large; acoustic; ...
$N \to ADJ\ N$	$IV \to$ performs; drinks; flies; ...
$VP \to IV$	$TV \to$ cuts; eats; plays; ...
$VP \to TV\ DP$	

Figure 1: CFG of the fragment of English in our data set

Adjective matrices are estimated from corpus-extracted examples of input noun vectors and the corresponding output adjective-noun phrase vectors, an idea also adopted by Guevara (2010).

The approach of Baroni and Zamparelli, termed `lexfunc` (because specific *lex*ical items act as *func*tors), is actually a specific instantiation of the DisCoCat formalism (Clark, 2012; Coecke et al., 2010), that looks at the general case of n-ary composition functions, encoded in higher-order tensors, with function application modeled by tensor contraction, a generalization of matrix-by-vector multiplication to tensors of arbitrary order. The DisCoCat approach has also been applied to transitive verbs by Grefenstette and Sadrzadeh (2011a) and Grefenstette and Sadrzadeh (2011b). The regression method proposed in Baroni and Zamparelli (2010) for estimating adjectives has been generalized by Grefenstette et al. (2013) and tested on transitive verbs modeled as two-argument functions (corresponding to third-order tensors).

3 Data set

We have built a data set of transitive and (a few) intransitive sentences that fall within the language recognized by the Context Free Grammar in Figure 1. As the rewriting rules of the grammar show, the subject and (in the case of transitive sentences) the object are always either a determiner phrase built by a determiner and a noun, where the noun can be optionally modified by one or more adjectives, or a bare noun phrase. The verb is always in the present tense and never negated. We use a total of 32 verbs, 7 determiners, 65 nouns, and 19 adjectives.

The data set is split into *paraphrase* and *foil sets*, described below. We use the term "paraphrase" to indicate that two sentences can describe essentially the same situation. The two subsets will be used to test DSMs in a paraphrase detection task, to understand which model better captures compositional meaning in natural language; the foil set, focusing on disruptive word order and determiner changes, has the purpose to help spotting whether a DSM is "cheating" in accomplishing this task, or, better, if it does detect paraphrases but does not properly capture compositionality.

Paraphrase set The sentences are grouped into sets of paraphrases. Some groups are rather similar to each other (for instance they are about someone playing some instrument) though they clearly describe a different situation (the player is a man vs. a woman or the instrument is a guitar vs. a violin), as it happens for the sentences in Group 1 and Group 2 listed in Table 1. We took as starting point the Microsoft Research Video Description Corpus (Chen and Dolan, 2011) considering only those sentences that could be simplified to fit in the CFG described above. We have obtained 20 groups of sentences. Groups which were left with just a few sentences after grammar-based trimming have been extended adding sentences with the nouns modified by an attributive adjective (chosen so that it would not distort the meaning of the sentence, e.g. we have added *tall* as modifier of *person* in "*A tall person makes a cake*", if there is no original sentence in the group that would describe the person differently), or adding sentences with a determiner similar to the one used in the original description (for instance *the* when there was *a*). In total, the set contains 157 sentences, divided into 20 groups; the smallest paraphrase group contains 4 sentences whereas the largest one consists of 17; the groups contain 7.85 sentences on average.

Group 1: Paraphrases	Group 2: Paraphrases
P A man plays a guitar P A man plays an acoustic guitar P A man plays an electric guitar P A old man plays guitar P The man plays the guitar P The man plays music P A man plays an instrument	P A girl plays violin P A lady plays violin P A woman plays violin P A woman plays the violin
Group 1: Foils	**Group 2: Foils**
S A guitar plays a man S An acoustic guitar plays a man S An instrument plays a man D No man plays no guitar SD No guitar plays no man SD No guitar plays a man D The man plays no guitar ...	S A violin plays a girl S A violin plays a lady ... D No girl plays violin D No lady plays violin

Table 1: Sample of paraphrases and foils of two groups

Foil set From each group in the paraphrase set, we have obtained foil paraphrase sentences in three ways: (i) by inverting the words in the subject and object position of the original sentences (sentences marked by S in Table 1); (ii) by replacing the determiner with a new one that clearly modifies the meaning of the sentences – replacing the original (positive) determiner with *no* (sentences marked by D); and by inverting subject and object of the sentences obtained by (ii) (sentences marked by SD). Note that the change in determiner, unlike in the case of the true paraphrase set above, is disruptive of meaning compatibility. In total there are 325 foils, the smallest group has 4 foils whereas the largest one consists of 36; on average the foil groups contain 17 sentences each.

4 Experiments

4.1 Semantic space and composition method implementation

We collect co-occurrence statistics from the concatenation of the ukWaC corpus,[2] a mid-2009 dump of the English Wikipedia[3] and the British National Corpus,[4] for a total of about 2.8 billion tokens. We extracted distributional vectors for the 20K most frequent inflected nouns in the corpus, and all the verbs, adjectives and determiners in the vocabulary of our data set (lemma forms). We adopt a bag-of-word approach, counting co-occurrence with all context words in the same sentence with a target item. Context words consist of the 10K most frequent lemmatized content words (nouns, adjectives, verbs, and adverbs). Raw frequencies are converted into Local Mutual Information scores (Evert, 2005), and the dimensions reduced to 200 by means of the Singular Value Decomposition.

For the *lexfunc* model, we used regression learning based on input and output examples automatically extracted from the corpus, along the lines of Baroni and Zamparelli (2010) and Grefenstette et al. (2013), in order to obtain tensors representing functor words in our vocabulary. Determiners, intransitive verbs and adjectives are treated as one-argument functions (second order tensors, or matrices) from nouns to determiner phrases, from determiner phrases to sentences, and from nouns to nouns, respectively. Transitive verbs are treated as two-argument functions (third order tensors) from determiner phrases to determiner phrases to sentences. For the multiplicative and additive models we consider two versions, one in

[2]`http://wacky.sslmit.unibo.it/`
[3]`http://en.wikipedia.org`
[4]`http://www.natcorp.ox.ac.uk/`

which determiners are ignored (as in Blacoe and Lapata, 2012) and one in which they are not. For *lexfunc* and the additive model, we also look at how normalizing the vectors to unit length before composition (both in training and testing) affects performance (*mult* is not affected by scalar transformations).

4.2 Evaluation methods

We have carried out two experiments. The first is a classic paraphrase detection task, in which CDSMs have to automatically cluster the sentences from the paraphrase set into the ground-truth groups. The second one aims to highlight when the possible good performance in the paraphrase detection task does correspond to true modelling of compositionality, that should be sensitive to word order and disruptive changes in the determiner.

Clustering We have carried out this experiment against the paraphrase set. We used the standard globally-optimized repeated bisecting method as implemented in the widely used CLUTO toolkit (Karypis, 2003), using cosines as distance functions, and accepting all of CLUTO's default values. Performance is measured by *purity*, one of the standard clustering quality measures returned by CLUTO (Zhao and Karypis, 2003). If n_r^i is the number of items from the *i*-th true (gold standard) group that were assigned to the *r*-th cluster, n is the total number of items and k the number of clusters, then: $Purity = \frac{1}{n}\sum_{r=1}^{k}\max_i(n_r^i)$. In the case of perfect clusters, purity will be of 100%; as cluster quality deteriorates, purity approaches 0.

Sentence similarity to paraphrases vs. foils The idea of the second experiment is to measure the similarity of each sentence in the paraphrase set to all other sentences in the same group (i.e., valid paraphrases, P), as well as to sentences in the corresponding foil set (FP). For each sentence in a P group, we computed the mean of the cosine of the sentence with all the sentences in the same ground-truth group (with all the P sentences) (`cos.para`) and the mean of the cosine with all the foil paraphrases (with all the FP sentences, viz. those marked by S, D, SD) of the same group (`cos.foil`). Then, we computed the difference between `cos.para` and `cos.foil` (`diff.para.foil= cos.para - cos.foil`). Finally, we computed the mean of `diff.para.foil` for all the sentences in the data set. Models which achieve higher values are those that are not captured by the foils' trap, since they are able to distinguish paraphrases from their foils: Only a model that realizes that *A man plays an instrument* is a better paraphrase of *A man plays guitar* than either *A guitar plays a man* or *The man plays no guitar* can be said to truly catch compositional meaning, beyond simple word meaning overlap. To focus more specifically on word order, we will report the same analysis also when considering only the scrambled sentences as foils: `diff.para.scrambled=cos.para - cos.scrambled`, where the latter are means of the cosine of the paraphrase with all the scrambled sentences (with all the sentences marked by S) of the same group (with no manipulation of the determiners).

4.3 Results

In Table 2 we report the performance of all the models evaluated with the two methods discussed above. Concerning the paraphrase clustering task, we first notice that all models are doing much better than the random baseline, and most of them are also above a challenging word-overlap baseline (challenging because sentences in the same groups do tend to share many words) (Kirschner et al., 2009). By far the highest purity value (0.84) was obtained by normalized *add* without determiners. This confirms that "shallow" approaches are indeed very good for paraphrase detection (Blacoe and Lapata, 2012). Interestingly, the additive model performs quite badly (0.32) if it is not normalized and determiners are not stripped off: A reasonable interpretation is that the determiner vectors tend to be both very long (determiners are very frequent) and uninformative (the same determiners occur in most sentences), so their impact must be dampened. Keeping determiners is also detrimental for the multiplicative model, that in general in our experiment does not perform as well as the additive one. The *lexfunc* model

Model	Experiment 1 Purity	Experiment 2 `diff.para.foil`	`diff.para.scrambled`
`mult`	0.49	0.05 (0.21)	0.04 (0.29)
`mult no det`	0.62	0.00 (0.19)	-0.01 (0.23)
`add`	0.32	0.12 (0.09)	0.00 (0.07)
`add norm`	0.78	0.06 (0.05)	0.00 (0.04)
`add no det`	0.74	0.00 (0.12)	0.01 (0.11)
`add norm no det`	**0.84**	0.00 (0.06)	0.00 (0.06)
`lexfunc`	0.59	**0.24** (0.25)	**0.28** (0.35)
`lexfunc norm`	0.75	0.06 (0.08)	0.09 (0.11)
`word overlap`	0.59		
`random`	0.11		

Table 2: Experiment results (mean `diff.para.foil` and `diff.para.scrambled` values followed by standard deviations)

without normalization performs at the level of the word-overlap baseline and the best multiplicative model, whereas its performance after normalization reaches that of *add* without determiners. Note that for *lexfunc*, normalization cannot be a way to lower the impact of determiners (that in this model are matrices, not vectors), so future work must ascertain why we observe this effect.

Coming now to the second experiment, we note that most models fell into the foils' trap. For neither multiplicative models the difference between similarity to true paraphrases vs. foils is significantly above zero (here and below, statistical significance measured by two-tailed t-tests). Among additive models, only those that do include information about determiners have differences between paraphrase and foil similarity significantly above zero. Indeed, since the additive model is by construction insensitive to word order, the fact that it displays a significant difference at all indicates that evidently the vectors representing determiners are more informative about their meaning than we thought. Still, we should remember that the only determiner replacement tested is the one from the positive determiners – *a*, *some*, *the*, *one*, *two*, *three* – to *no*. Further studies on the role of determiners in the distributional meaning of sentences should be carried out, before any strong conclusion can be drawn. Finally, both *lexfunc* models display paraphrase-foil differences significantly above zero, and the non-normalized model in particular works very well in this setting (being also significantly better than the second best, namely the *add* model).

The comparison of the values obtained for `diff.para.foil` and `diff.para.scrambled` is only interesting for the *lexfunc* models. Remember that the latter comparison tells us which models fail to compose meaning because they are insensitive to word order, whereas the former also takes determiners into account. Since *mult* and *add* do not take word order into account, they of course have values of `diff.para.scrambled` that are not significantly different from 0 (consider this a sanity check!). Both *lexfunc* variants have values for this variable that are significantly higher than 0, showing that this model is not only taking word order into account, but making good use of this information.

To conclude, all compositional models perform paraphrase clustering quite well, and indeed on this task a simple additive model performs best. However, the picture changes if instead of considering groups of paraphrases extracted from a standard paraphrase data set, we look at a task where paraphrases must be distinguished by foils that are deliberately constructed to take the effect of determiners and word order into account. In this setup, only the *lexfunc* model is consistently performing above chance level. Still, since the version of *lexfunc* that handles the second task best only performs paraphrase clustering at the level of the word-overlap baseline, we cannot really claim that this is a satisfactory model of compositional sentence meaning, and clearly further work is called for to test and develop better compositional distributional semantic models.

5 Conclusion

We have proposed a new method for evaluating Compositional Distributional Models (CDSMs) that we believe can get a more reliable fingerprint of how different CDSMs are capturing compositionality. Turney (2012) has proposed to create foil paraphrases of phrases by switching the word order (often resulting in ungrammatical sequences). We have extended the method to sentential paraphrases (while guaranteeing grammaticality) and have added a new trap for the CDSMs, namely determiner replacement. Starting from the Microsoft Research video description corpus, we have developed a data set organized in groups of paraphrases and foils (obtained by both word order switch and determiner replacement) and evaluated the performance of several CDSMs against it. None of the models can be claimed to be the successful one, since the additive model is best in capturing paraphrase clustering, whereas the *lexfunc* model is best in distinguishing sentences involving word order switch and the effect of determiners. For the future, we might consider the possibility of investigating an hybrid system that combines insights from these two models. Furthermore, the current data set does not provide enough variety in meaning-preserving and disruptive determiner changes to single out the effect of determiners like we did for word order, hence further studies in this direction are required. All in all, we believe the evaluation confirms the need of setting up semantic tasks suitable for evaluating the real challenges CDSMs are said to be tackling. We hope that the data set we developed can be a step in this direction. To this extent, we make it publicly available from `http://clic.cimec.unitn.it/composes/`.

Acknowledgments

The work has been funded by the ERC 2011 Starting Independent Research Grant supporting the COMPOSES project (nr. 283554).

References

Baroni, M., R. Bernardi, N.-Q. Do, and C.-C. Shan (2012). Entailment above the word level in distributional semantics. In *Proceedings of EACL*, Avignon, France, pp. 23–32.

Baroni, M. and R. Zamparelli (2010). Nouns are vectors, adjectives are matrices: Representing adjective-noun constructions in semantic space. In *Proceedings of EMNLP*, Boston, MA, pp. 1183–1193.

Blacoe, W. and M. Lapata (2012). A comparison of vector-based representations for semantic composition. In *Proceedings of EMNLP*, Jeju Island, Korea, pp. 546–556.

Chen, D. L. and W. B. Dolan (2011). Collecting highly parallel data for paraphrase evaluation. In *Proceedings of ACL*, Portland, OR, pp. 190–200.

Clark, S. (2012). Type-driven syntax and semantics for composing meaning vectors. In C. Heunen, M. Sadrzadeh, and E. Grefenstette (Eds.), *Quantum Physics and Linguistics: A Compositional, Diagrammatic Discourse*. Oxford, UK: Oxford University Press. In press.

Coecke, B., M. Sadrzadeh, and S. Clark (2010). Mathematical foundations for a compositional distributional model of meaning. *Linguistic Analysis 36*, 345–384.

Dolan, W., C. Quirk, and C. Brockett (2004). Unsupervised construction of large paraphrase corpora: Exploiting massively parallel news sources. In *Proceedings of COLING*, pp. 350–356.

Evert, S. (2005). *The Statistics of Word Cooccurrences*. Dissertation, Stuttgart University.

Grefenstette, E., G. Dinu, Y.-Z. Zhang, M. Sadrzadeh, and M. Baroni (2013). Multi-step regression learning for compositional distributional semantics. In *Proceedings of IWCS*, Potsdam, Germany. In press.

Grefenstette, E. and M. Sadrzadeh (2011a). Experimental support for a categorical compositional distributional model of meaning. In *Proceedings of EMNLP*, Edinburgh, UK, pp. 1394–1404.

Grefenstette, E. and M. Sadrzadeh (2011b). Experimenting with transitive verbs in a DisCoCat. In *Proceedings of GEMS*, Edinburgh, UK, pp. 62–66.

Griffiths, T., M. Steyvers, and J. Tenenbaum (2007). Topics in semantic representation. *Psychological Review 114*, 211–244.

Guevara, E. (2010). A regression model of adjective-noun compositionality in distributional semantics. In *Proceedings of GEMS*, Uppsala, Sweden, pp. 33–37.

Karypis, G. (2003). CLUTO: A clustering toolkit. Technical Report 02-017, University of Minnesota Department of Computer Science.

Kintsch, W. (2001). Predication. *Cognitive Science 25*(2), 173–202.

Kirschner, M., R. Bernardi, . Baroni, and L. T. Dinh (2009). Analyzing interactive QA dialogues using logistic regression models. In *Proceedings of AI*IA*, pp. 334–344.

Landauer, T. and S. Dumais (1997). A solution to Plato's problem: The latent semantic analysis theory of acquisition, induction, and representation of knowledge. *Psychological Review 104*(2), 211–240.

Lund, K. and C. Burgess (1996). Producing high-dimensional semantic spaces from lexical co-occurrence. *Behavior Research Methods 28*, 203–208.

McDonald, S. (2000). *Environmental Determinants of Lexical Processing Effort*. Ph. D. thesis, University of Edinburgh.

Mitchell, J. and M. Lapata (2008). Vector-based models of semantic composition. In *Proceedings of ACL*, Columbus, OH, pp. 236–244.

Mitchell, J. and M. Lapata (2009). Language models based on semantic composition. In *Proceedings of EMNLP*, Singapore, pp. 430–439.

Mitchell, J. and M. Lapata (2010). Composition in distributional models of semantics. *Cognitive Science 34*(8), 1388–1429.

Socher, R., E. Huang, J. Pennin, A. Ng, and C. Manning (2011). Dynamic pooling and unfolding recursive autoencoders for paraphrase detection. In *Proceedings of NIPS*, Granada, Spain, pp. 801–809.

Socher, R., B. Huval, C. Manning, and A. Ng (2012). Semantic compositionality through recursive matrix-vector spaces. In *Proceedings of EMNLP*, Jeju Island, Korea, pp. 1201–1211.

Turney, P. (2012). Domain and function: A dual-space model of semantic relations and compositions. *Journal of Artificial Intelligence Research 44*, 533–585.

Zhao, Y. and G. Karypis (2003). Criterion functions for document clustering: Experiments and analysis. Technical Report 01-40, University of Minnesota Department of Computer Science.

The Curious Case of Metonymic Verbs: A Distributional Characterization

Jason Utt[1], Alessandro Lenci[2], Sebastian Padó[3], Alessandra Zarcone[1]
[1]Universität Stuttgart, [2]Universität Heidelberg, [3]Università di Pisa
[1]uttjn,zarconaa@ims.uni-stuttgart.de,
[2]alessandro.lenci@ling.unipi.it, [3]pado@cl.uni-heidelberg.de

Abstract

Logical metonymy combines an event-selecting verb with an entity-denoting noun (e.g., *The writer began the novel*), triggering a covert event interpretation (e.g., *reading*, *writing*). Experimental investigations of logical metonymy must assume a binary distinction between metonymic (i.e. event-selecting) verbs and non-metonymic verbs to establish a control condition. However, this binary distinction (whether a verb is metonymic or not) is mostly made on intuitive grounds, which introduces a potential confounding factor.

We describe a corpus-based approach which characterizes verbs in terms of their behavior at the syntax-semantics interface. The model assesses the extent to which transitive verbs prefer event-denoting objects over entity-denoting objects. We then test this "eventhood" measure on psycholinguistic datasets, showing that it can distinguish not only metonymic from non-metonymic verbs, but that it can also capture more fine-grained distinctions among different classes of metonymic verbs, putting such distinctions into a new graded perspective.

1 Motivation

Logical metonymy, an instance of *enriched composition* (Jackendoff, 1997), consists of a combination of an event-selecting metonymic verb and an entity-denoting direct (e.g., *The writer began the novel*).[1] Its interpretation involves the recovery of a *covert event* (*reading*, *writing*). Metonymy interpretation is generally explained in terms of a type clash between the verb's selectional restrictions and the noun's type, and extensive psycholinguistic work (McElree et al. (2001) and Traxler et al. (2002), among others) has demonstrated extra processing costs for metonymic constructions. For example, Traxler et al. (2002) combine metonymic and non-metonymic verbs with entity-denoting and event-denoting nouns (*The boy [started/saw]$_V$ [the puzzle/fight]$_{NP}$*) and report significantly higher processing costs for the "coercion combination" (metonymic verb plus entity-denoting object: *The boy started the puzzle*).

While there has been much debate in theoretical linguistics on individual verbs that may or may not give rise to logical metonymy (for example, on *enjoy*, see Pustejovsky (1995); Fodor and Lepore (1998); Lascarides and Copestake (1998)), work in psycholinguistics (McElree et al., 2001; Traxler et al., 2002; Pylkkänen and McElree, 2006) and computational modeling (Lapata et al., 2003; Lapata and Lascarides, 2003) seem to have agreed on a small set of "metonymic verbs" which is used when looking for empirical correlates of logical metonymy. However, this set of metonymic verbs is semantically rather heterogeneous, as it is selected based on intuition only. It includes not only aspectual verbs[2] (*begin*, *complete*, *continue*, *end*, *finish*, *start*) but also psychological verbs (*enjoy*, *hate*, *like*, *love*, *regret*, *savor*, *try*), as well as others that elude straightforward categorization (*attempt*, *endure*, *manage*, *master*, *prefer*).

[1]In this paper we follow the accepted broad linguistic-philosophical distinction between "events" and "(physical) objects" (Casati and Varzi, 2010), using the term "entity" to refer to the ontological class of "object" as opposed to "event". This is to avoid confusion with the grammatical function of "object".

[2]We use the terminology of Levin (1993).

This semantic heterogeneity calls into question a homogeneous notion of metonymic verbs. Indeed, recent work by Katsika et al. (2012) notes that "the hypothesis that eventive inferences must be attributed to the same mechanism of building meaning (coercion + type-shifting) [for all metonymic verbs] is too strong". Their eye-tracking study supports the hypothesis that aspectual verbs trigger coercion and processing cost, while psychological predicates (e.g. *enjoy*) do not. This gives rise a key question: *Are all metonymic verbs alike?*

A second potential methodological risk arises from the fact that experiments need to pair metonymic verbs with a control group of non-metonymic verbs. Verbs that are typically used as non-metonymic include *forget*, *recall*, *remember*, *describe*, *praise*, *prepare*, *shelve*, *see*, and *unpack*. The demarcation of metonymic vs. non-metonymic verbs is rarely motivated explicitly and in some cases even seems rather arbitrary. This raises an evident risk of circularity: the definition of logical metonymy relies on the notion of metonymic verbs, but this class is often characterized only in terms of their triggering metonymic shifts. What is needed is a set of independent and principled criteria to approach what we feel is a second crucial question: *What is a metonymic verb?*

In this paper, we make some progress towards answering these questions by proposing a corpus-based measure of *eventhood* that captures the degree to which verbs expect objects that are events rather than entities. This measure is able to: (a) distinguish between aspectual metonymic verbs, non-aspectual metonymic verbs, and non-metonymic verbs, lending support to Katsika et al.'s (2012) argument; (b) provide empirical evidence for or against the choice of materials in psycholinguistic studies of metonymy; (c) serve as a necessary (although not sufficient) indicator of new verbs that might show metonymic behavior.

Plan of the paper. Section 2 describes the the definition of our eventhood measure ϵ and uses it for data exploration. Section 3 characterizes the data used in two psycholinguistic studies on metonymy. Our results show that our measure can distinguish verb classes, reliably predicting participants' behavior in the experiments.

2 Measuring the Event Expectations of Verbs

Our starting point is that metonymic verbs should be statistically more associated with event-denoting objects, while the non-metonymic verbs should mainly co-occur with entity-denoting objects. We move on to define a measure of "eventhood" of a verb's object slot[3] and to use it to distinguish between verb classes. Our hypotheses are that (a) aspectual verbs have a higher eventhood score than entity-selecting verbs and (b) aspectual verbs have a higher eventhood-score than non-aspectual metonymic verbs.

2.1 Selection of typical objects from corpus data

There has been much work on modeling the various fillers of verbs, i.e. their *selectional preferences*, using explicit or implicit generalizations of the fillers. These rely either primarily on a lexical hierarchy (Resnik, 1996), distributional information (Rooth et al., 1999; Erk et al., 2010) or both (Schulte im Walde et al., 2008). While such computationally-intensive approaches have proven effective in modeling selectional preferences in general, we are interested in learning about only one aspect of a verb's argument, namely how 'event-like' it is.

We use the WordNet (Fellbaum, 2010)[4] lexical hierarchy to discover whether a noun has an event sense. We also use Distributional Memory (DM, Baroni and Lenci (2010)) as a source of distributional information that allows us to determine how strongly a noun is associated with a given verb as an object filler. DM is a general distributional semantic resource which allows the generation of vector-based semantic models (Turney and Pantel, 2010) from the distribution of words in context. In general, distributional semantic models are two-dimensional, relating a word with other words in its context giving

[3]We will subsequently simplify the terminology and speak of a "verb's eventhood."

[4]We use version 3 of WordNet, available at: `http://wordnet.princeton.edu/wordnet/download`.

a 'bag-of-words' model (Schütze (1993), cf. Table 1 (a)); or with particular syntactic patterns to give a 'structured vector space' (Padó and Lapata (2007), cf. Table 1 (b)).

(a)	***dog***:	*cat*:40.2 *bone*:25.1 *best*:10.3 …
	cat:	*milk*:37.3 …
	⋮	
(b)	***dog***:	$\langle obj, pet\rangle$:30.2 $\langle subj, bark\rangle$:20.4 $\langle subj, bite\rangle$:7.5 …
	cat:	$\langle subj, purr\rangle$:25.2 …
	⋮	

Table 1: Examples of a two-dimensional bag-of-words space (a), and a two-dimensional structured space (b).

DM is a three-dimensional extension of such a two-dimensional matrix which includes the syntactically derived relation between the two words as an extra dimension. It is derived from the concatenation of the ukWaC[5], the English Wikipedia[6], and the BNC[7], resulting altogether in a 2.83 billion-token corpus. We use the TypeDM variant of DM,[8] which contains over 130M links between nouns, verbs and adjectives, covering generic syntactic relations as well as lexicalized relations (see Baroni and Lenci (2010) for details). In DM, each triple of words w_1, w_2 and relation r, $\langle w_1\ r\ w_2\rangle$, is scored by the Local Mutual Information (LMI, Evert (2005), Equation 1) between its three elements. LMI contains two factors, (i) the point-wise mutual information which indicates how strongly their co-occurrence deviates from chance and (ii) the raw co-occurrence frequency:

$$LMI = O_{w_1,r,w_2} \cdot log\frac{O_{w_1,r,w_2}}{E_{w_1,r,w_2}}, \qquad (1)$$

where $E_.$ is the MLE-expected frequency of the triple, and $O_.$ its actually observed frequency in the corpus. For example, since the LMI score for ⟨*meeting obj postpone*⟩ is greater than that for ⟨*breakfast obj postpone*⟩ we can say that *breakfast* is a less typical object for *postpone* than *meeting*. Defined in this manner, typicality is not only a function of the co-occurrence frequency between an object and a verb but of the significance of this co-occurrence compared to chance. The format of DM allows for the simple extraction of highly informative fillers for a given verb by selecting those tuples whose relation is the one of interest and sorting by score. In the following sections we will use the standard matricization of DM (W×LW) as a semantic space, which defines as dimensions the pairs of links and context words as in Table 1 (b).

2.2 Defining event nouns in a lexical hierarchy

In order to determine how event-like the typical object is for a given predicate, we have to distinguish which objects have an event sense. We define an event noun as a noun with at least one WordNet synset (Fellbaum, 2010) that is dominated in the synset hierarchy by one of the top nodes shown in Table 2. This is a simple approximation of the degree to which the noun denotes an event. A more informed measure could e.g. include distributional information of the noun's senses. It is important to note that a particular noun can have more than one event-dominated synset. There are in fact eight nouns whose synsets generalize to all of the event nodes designated:

control, culture, differentiation, elimination, inspiration, pleasure, reproduction, rumination,

that is, they all have an *action, cognitive process*, and *biological process* reading.

[5] `http://wacky.sslmit.unibo.it`
[6] `http://en.wikipedia.org`
[7] `http://www.natcorp.ox.ac.uk`
[8] TypeDM is available from `http://clic.cimec.unitn.it/dm/`.

WordNet node	Count	Examples
EVENT	11248	*training, splat, Alamo, suicide, hyperalimentation*
ACT/DEED/HUMAN ACTION/HUMAN ACTIVITY, ACTION, ACTIVITY	9845	*banditry, dissolution, beanball, messaging, banishment*
PROCESS/PHYSICAL PROCESS	2590	*ultracentrifugation, desensitisation, extinction, superconductivity*
PROCESS/COGNITIVE PROCESS/MENTAL PROCESS /OPERATION/COGNITIVE OPERATION	998	*reminiscence, breakdown, score, analogy, inference*
ORGANIC PROCESS/BIOLOGICAL PROCESS	878	*recuperation, emission, autoregulation, drinking, blossoming*
all	14143	

Table 2: High-level event-denoting nodes in WordNet with examples.

This definition leads to a set EV of 14K event nouns (out of WordNet's 170K nouns), which we can use to determine to what extent 'the typical object' of a verb is event-like. First we take the k most strongly associated object fillers from DM, $obj_k(v)$ for the verb v and then define the eventhood to be the percentage of these fillers that have an event sense. In other words, the eventhood ϵ_k for a verb v is defined as:

$$\epsilon_k(v) = \frac{|EV \cap obj_k(v)|}{k}. \quad (2)$$

Selecting the top k scored fillers as prototypical arguments has proven a reliable method to characterize the expectations for the argument slot which allows, e.g., the modeling of selectional preferences (cf. Baroni and Lenci (2010); Erk et al. (2010); Lenci (2011)). For the present analysis, we fix k at 100 (i.e. $\epsilon := \epsilon_{100}$), we thereby also eliminate the issue of using words from DM which are not covered in WordNet. The following section investigates the range of eventhood scores across the verbs in DM.

2.3 Evaluation on Verbs in DM

Figure 1 shows the distribution of eventhood across verbs in DM. Verbs with $\epsilon \approx 0$, i.e. verbs with low eventhood, include *unfrock, detain, marry,* and *behead*, while verbs with high eventhood, i.e. those which rank the highest with respect to ϵ (i.e. $\epsilon \approx 1$), include *expedite, undergo, halt,* and *delay*.

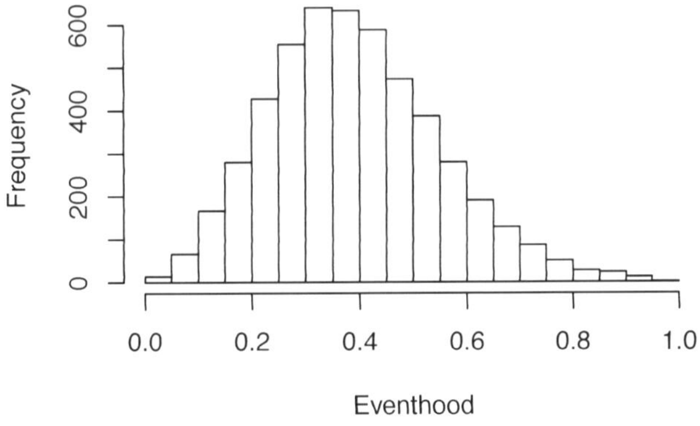

Figure 1: Histogram of eventhood across verbs in DM.

While this 'linearization' of the space of verbs given by their eventhood scores does not in and of itself suggest semantic coherence—given a particular range $[\alpha; \beta]$, the class of verbs with $\alpha < \epsilon(v) < \beta$ will in general be a heterogenous class—we find that in the fringe ranges, i.e. where $\epsilon \approx 0$ and $\epsilon \approx 1$, the verbs appear to be coherent with respect to their object fillers. For instance, the left most bar in the histogram corresponding to the range $0 < \epsilon < 0.5$ typically have people as the experiencers of the action denoted by the verb. In a sense, things that happen to or with people (e.g. *marry* or *behead*) do not typically happen to or with events. On the other side of the spectrum we have only 13 verbs with $0.9 < \epsilon < 1$ (e.g. *commence, cease, halt, delay*), most of which concern the temporal unfolding of an event.

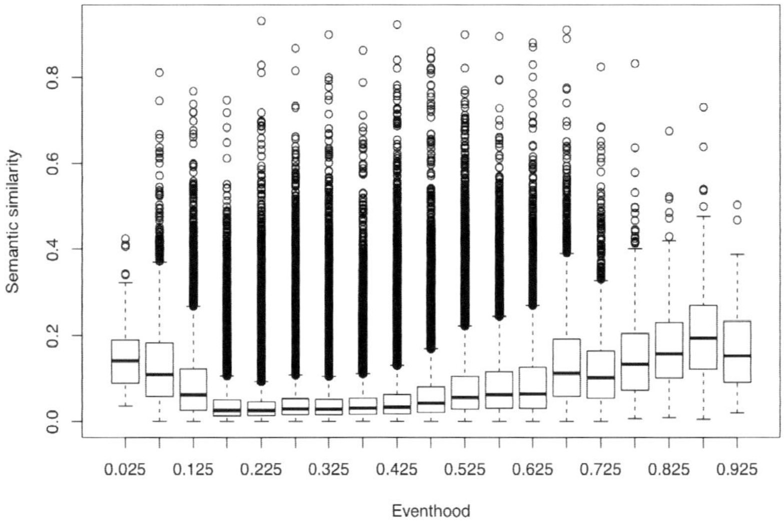

Figure 2: Pairwise semantic similarity within $\{v|\alpha < \epsilon(v) < \beta\}$ in DM.

The most frequent range ($0.3 < \epsilon < 0.35$), covering 640 verbs, contains a very diverse group of verbs: *prance, fluoridate, emaciate* ($\epsilon \approx 0.3$) to *exorcise, downsize, muddy* ($\epsilon \approx 0.35$). To determine the semantic coherence across eventhood scores, we computed the pairwise cosine semantic similarity between the verbs within each eventhood range (Figure 1). Figure 2 shows the semantic similarities among verbs for each bin in the range $[\alpha; \beta]$. The similarities for each set of n verbs $\{v|\alpha < \epsilon(v) < \beta\}$ were then contrasted with the pairwise similarities for n randomly drawn verbs. In 19 out of the 20 bins the actual verb similarities were statistically higher than the random ones ($p < .001$). This means that the verbs within each range form a semantically coherent group, suggesting that the eventhood score can identify semantically related verbs.

Towards either end of the eventhood spectrum (Figure 2), we see that the verbs are semantically much more similar to one another, while the mid-range is the most semantically dissimilar. In the extreme cases, we are dealing with verbs that are similar to one another, while in the mid-range the semantic coherence is lost.

3 Evaluation on Psycholinguistic Datasets

We test our model on the experimental datasets from two metonymy interpretation studies (Traxler et al., 2002; Katsika et al., 2012). Each of these studies makes use of a classification, according to which it expects participants' behavior to differ. More precisely, they expect more difficulty in processing when 'metonymic' verbs are combined with non-event denoting objects than when 'less metonymic' verbs are.

If, as those studies claim, event-selecting verbs give rise to higher processing costs when combined with entity-denoting objects, then we expect our eventhood measure to be able to distinguish between the classes used in the psycholinguistic studies.

Traxler et al.'s (2002) dataset	metonymic	begin, complete, end, endure, enjoy, expect, finish, prefer, start
	non-metonymic	approve, curse, describe, forget, ignore, observe, outline, praise, prepare, recall, recollect, remember, report, see, watch
Katsika et al.'s (2012) dataset	metonymic aspectual	begin, complete, continue, finish, start
	metonymic psychological	enjoy, face, favor, prefer, resist, stomach, tolerate
	non-metonymic	access, auction, buy, conduct, contribute, deliver, destroy, drop, fax,find, inspect, misplace, open, peruse, purchase, photocopy, rent, sell, send, shelve, shred, submit, trash, unearth, unpack, write

Table 3: Datasets from Traxler et al. (2002) and Katsika et al. (2012).

3.1 The Datasets

The two datasets used are:

Traxler et al. (2002) dataset: composed of 24 verbs used in Experiment 2 and 3 in Traxler et al. (2002). Verbs are divided in *metonymic* and *non-metonymic* verbs (*event verbs* and *neutral verbs*, according to the terminology of the study). Higher processing costs were yielded for metonymic verbs combined with entity-denoting objects than for all remaining conditions (metonymic verbs combined with event-denoting objects and non-metonymic verbs combined with entity and event-denoting objects).

Katsika et al. (2012) dataset: composed of 38 verbs used in Katsika et al. (2012) taken mostly from previous psycholinguistic experiments on type-shifting.[9] As mentioned above, Katsika et al. (2012) make a point of distinguishing between three sets of verbs: here *metonymic aspectual*, *metonymic psychological* and *non-metonymic* verbs. (according to the terminology of the study, *aspectual*, *psychological* and *entity-selecting*). Readers spent more time re-reading the verb in the metonymic aspectual condition than the metonymic psychological or non-metonymic condition.

3.2 Evaluation

A direct correlation between eventhood and reading times is not feasible, because the psycholinguistic studies do not report reading times for each verb, but rather the average per condition (and even if they did, the number of measurements per verb would be too small). Thus, we resort to two alternative evaluation methods:

1. For both datasets, we report the Wilcoxon rank sum test (a non-parametric analog of Student's t-test) to check for differences in eventhood between verb classes.
2. In Traxler et al.'s (2002) dataset, each sentence exists once with a metonymic verb and once with a non-metonymic verb, which gives us a list of verb pairs. This list allows us to compute the number of times the eventhood of the metonymic verb is higher than the eventhood of the non-metonymic verb.

[9] The study also used verbs that do not select for a direct object. We excluded these.

metonymic		non-metonymic		prediction
verb	eventhood	verb	eventhood	correct?
begin	0.91	praise	0.55	y
complete	0.79	recall	0.67	y
start	0.78	see	0.51	y
endure	0.73	report	0.78	n
end	0.72	outline	0.64	y
finish	0.66	prepare	0.41	y
enjoy	0.57	watch	0.60	n
enjoy	0.57	curse	0.31	y
prefer	0.54	praise	0.55	n

Table 4: Eventhood values for some verb pairs from Traxler et al. (2002) and correctness of model prediction.

3.3 Results

We first consider the Katsika et al. (2012) data. Metonymic aspectual verbs yield higher eventhood scores compared to metonymic psychological verbs and non-metonymic verbs. All pairwise comparisons are significant: metonymic aspectual verbs vs. metonymic psychological verbs ($W = 30, p < 0.05$); metonymic aspectual verbs vs. non-metonymic verbs ($W = 125, p < 0.01$); metonymic psychological vs. non-metonymic verbs ($W = 18.5, p < 0.01$).

For the Traxler et al. (2002) dataset, the difference between metonymic verbs and non-metonymic verbs is close to significance, with p just above 0.05 ($W = 100.5, p < 0.053$). The fact that this difference is less significant is compatible with the observations in Katsika et al. (2012), namely that the set of verbs typically used in studies on logical metonymy is heterogeneous and includes verbs which are less event-selecting than aspectual verbs. In fact, if we remove the four metonymic verbs that are not aspectual (*endure, enjoy, expect, prefer*), we find a significant difference between the non-metonymical and metonymic (now aspectual-only) classes ($W = 67.5, p < 0.01$).

On the Traxler et al. (2002) dataset, the model scores 23/32 in the pairwise comparisons. In other words, metonymic verbs receive higher eventhood scores for 72 % of the pairs. Table 4 shows some examples of the pairwise comparisons. We find that errors tend to occur for metonymic psychological verbs more often than for metonymic aspectual verbs. The reason is that the most event-affine non-metonymic verbs (*recall, report*) prefer events to a higher degree than the least event-affine metonymic verbs (*enjoy, prefer*). This again suggests that Traxler et al.'s (2002) set of metonymic verbs is not clearly distinct from their non-metonymic verbs. This point is reinforced by Figure 3 which visualizes the eventhood distributions for the verb classes in both datasets as density plots and boxplots. The more homogeneous three-class distinctions in Katsika et al. (2012) seems justified as it clearly identifies three different selection behaviors (metonymic aspectual, metonymic psychological, non-metonymic), while the two-class distinction in Traxler et al. (2002) shows substantial overlap.

3.4 Discussion

Our results indicate that eventhood is a good indicator of 'metonymicity' and can even distinguish between classes of metonymic verbs. This raises the question of how strong the correlation between metonymicity and eventhood really is.

A first question is whether verbs need to have an (almost) perfect eventhood score to be metonymic. This is not plausible: if a verb is metonymic, we expect it to allow for entity-denoting objects, even if they will occur less frequently. For instance, *begin* is, arguably, a 'true' metonymic verb (metonymic aspectual). However, occurrences of *begin* in metonymical context (with entity objects) are indeed attested in the

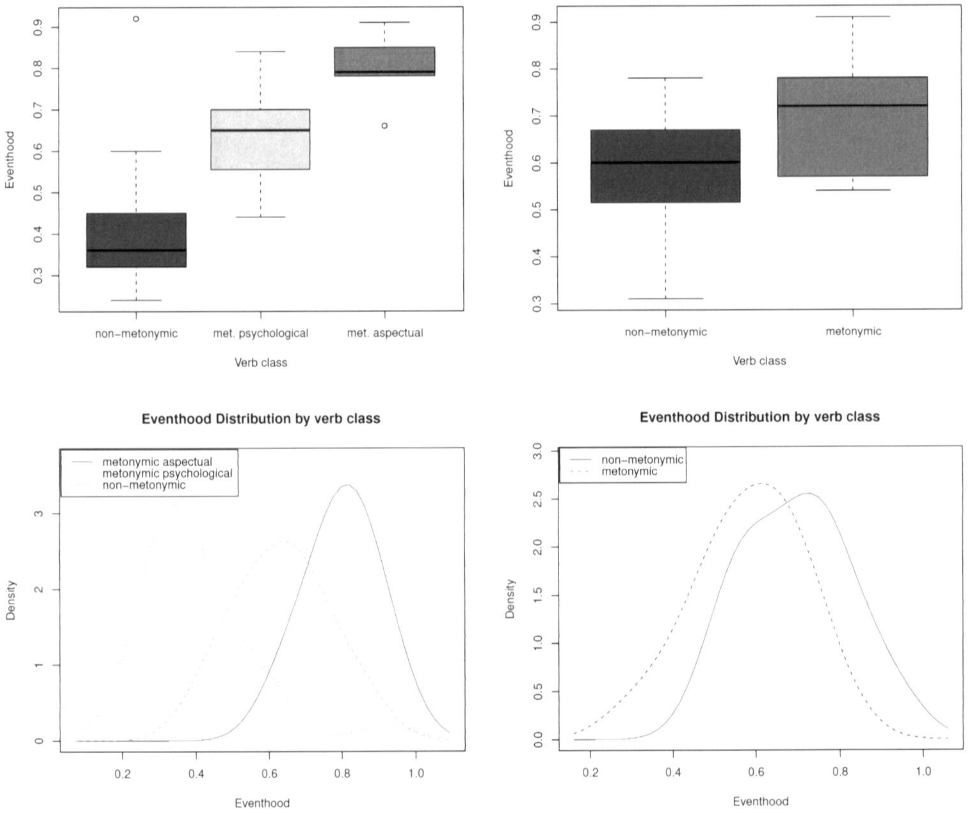

Figure 3: Comparing eventhood distribution for verb classes in the Katsika et al. (2012) dataset (left) and Traxler et al. (2002) dataset (right).

corpus. Consequently, it obtains an eventhood score of 0.91. Generally, we expect metonymic verbs to be placed at the high end of the eventhood spectrum, but not at the extreme (cf. Figure 3).

A second question is whether all verbs at the upper end of the eventhood range are (or at least can be) metonymic. Our inspection shows that verbs with an extremely high eventhood tend to disprefer metonymic constructions. Among the top eventhood-scoring verbs are, for instance, *perform, undergo, protest, conduct, spearhead, facilitate, undertake, witness*. All of these verbs clearly prefer events and occur infrequently in metonymic constructions. However, occasional metonymic productivity occurs, as in the following examples from American discussion forums on the web:

> There's a huge connection between Prematurity and GBS morbidities and mortalities and I too would be more then willing to undergo the antibiotics if such a risk factor was involved.

> *[The Adventures of Tom Sawyer]* is called the first real work of the American Literature movement, which in general spawned the Hemingways and Faulkners I would later undertake.

> Taking an IPD approach, we collaborated with Zeemac using 3D modeling known as "real time design" to facilitate the floor plan.

In sum, the correlation between eventhood and metonymicity is strong but not perfect. It remains a question for further investigation which other factors are involved in determining whether a high-eventhood verb features prominently in metonymic constructions (*begin*) or not (*conduct*). One factor that we want to investigate is *specificity*, following the intuition that only verbs that refer to general properties of as many events as possible (like aspectual properties) rather than specific scenarios are suitable as metonymic verbs.

4 Conclusions

In this paper, we have introduced a simple data-driven measure of *eventhood*, that is, the degree to which verbs prefer events over entities as their direct objects. Our eventhood measure allows us to characterize and separate verb classes relevant for logical metonymy that were so far hand-picked on the basis of intuitive considerations.

The fundamentally graded nature of our measure suggests that there is no clear-cut binary distinction between metonymic verbs on one end and non-metonymic verbs on the other. Instead, there is a continuum with a sequence of classes (named in decreasing order of eventhood): First, verbs with an extremely high eventhood such as *undergo* strongly disprefer entity-denoting objects, but in some creative uses they may still combine with them giving rise to metonymic interpretation. Next, metonymic aspectual verbs strongly prefer event-denoting objects but are (albeit less frequently) attested with entity-denoting objects and form "classic" cases of metonymy. Psychological verbs have a less strong bias for event-denoting objects, but can still be considered as metonymic (although, as Katsika et al. (2012) argue, with their own behavioral patterns). Finally, there is the wide range of non-metonymic verbs that are either neutral or entity-prefering.

This picture indicates that the question of how to select verbs for the control condition against which metonymical verbs are compared is by no means trivial. We believe that our depiction of the metonymic behavior as a graded range suggests that eventhood can be used to inform and guide the design of further materials in this area.

In closing, we note that expectations for the semantic types (event/entity) of verbal arguments can be understood as a very coarse variant of selectional preferences, and our model as a much simplified version of ontological models of selectional preferences (Resnik, 1996). On the other hand, the existence of classes with graded preferences indicates that eventhood differences may not be binary distinctions, but that we might rather be dealing with a graded range of behaviors. This has clear consequences for type-clash accounts of logical metonymy: given the existence of many verbs which exhibit intermediate behavior, it seems unlikely that there are two exclusive classes (metonymic vs. non-metonymic). Within this graded picture, the function of the type clash may be taken over by mismatches between preference (expectation) for an object and the actually encountered object.

The preliminary investigations presented in this paper thus show that corpus data can be used to provide independent empirical grounding to theory-loaded notions such as the one of metonymic verbs. This can be extremely useful for future experimental work as well as to evaluate experimental results.

Acknowledgements The research for this paper was funded by the German Research Foundation (Deutsche Forschungsgemeinschaft) as part of the SFB 732 "Incremental specification in context" / project D6 "Lexical-semantic factors in event interpretation" at the University of Stuttgart.

References

Baroni, M. and A. Lenci (2010). Distributional memory: A general framework for corpus-based semantics. *Computational Linguistics 36*(4), 1–49.

Casati, R. and A. C. Varzi (2010). Events. In N. Zalta (Ed.), *The Stanford Encyclopedia of Philosophy*. http://plato.stanford.edu/archives/spr2010/entries/events/.

Erk, K., S. Padó, and U. Padó (2010). A flexible, corpus-driven model of regular and inverse selectional preferences. *Computational Linguistics 36*(4), 723–763.

Evert, S. (2005). *The Statistics of Word Co-Occurrences: Word Pairs and Collocations*. Ph. D. thesis, Institut für Maschinelle Sprachverarbeitung, Universität Stuttgart.

Fellbaum, C. (2010). Wordnet. *Theory and Applications of Ontology: Computer Applications*, 231–243.

Fodor, J. and E. Lepore (1998). The emptiness of the lexicon: reflections on James Pustejovsky's The Generative Lexicon. *Linguistic Inquiry 29*(2), 269–288.

Jackendoff, R. (1997). *The Architecture of the Language Faculty*. MIT Press.

Katsika, A., D. Braze, A. Deo, and M. Piñango (2012). Complement coercion: Distinguishing between type-shifting and pragmatic inferencing. *The Mental Lexicon 7*(1), 58–76.

Lapata, M., F. Keller, and C. Scheepers (2003). Intra-sentential context effects on the interpretation of logical metonymy. *Cognitive Science 27*(4), 649–668.

Lapata, M. and A. Lascarides (2003). A probabilistic account of logical metonymy. *Computational Linguistics 29*(2), 263–317.

Lascarides, A. and A. Copestake (1998). Pragmatics and word meaning. *Journal of Linguistics 34*(02), 387–414.

Lenci, A. (2011). Composing and updating verb argument expectations: A distributional semantic model. In *Proceedings of the 2nd Workshop on Cognitive Modeling and Computational Linguistics*, Portland, Oregon, pp. 58–66.

Levin, B. (1993). *English verb classes and alternations: A preliminary investigation*, Volume 348. University of Chicago press Chicago, IL.

McElree, B., M. Traxler, M. Pickering, R. Seely, and R. Jackendoff (2001). Reading time evidence for enriched composition. *Cognition 78*(1), B17–B25.

Padó, S. and M. Lapata (2007). Dependency-based construction of semantic space models. *Computational Linguistics 33*(2), 161–199.

Pustejovsky, J. (1995). *The Generative Lexicon*. MIT Press.

Pylkkänen, L. and B. McElree (2006). The syntax-semantic interface: On-line composition of sentence meaning. In *Handbook of Psycholinguistics*, pp. 537–577. Elsevier.

Resnik, P. (1996). Selectional constraints: an information-theoretic model and its computational realization.

Rooth, M., S. Riezler, D. Prescher, G. Carroll, and F. Beil (1999). Inducing a Semantically Annotated Lexicon via EM-Based Clustering. In *Proceedings of the 37th Annual Meeting of the Association for Computational Linguistics*, Maryland, MD.

Schulte im Walde, S., C. Hying, C. Scheible, and H. Schmid (2008). Combining EM training and the MDL principle for an automatic verb classification incorporating selectional preferences. In *Proc. of ACL*, pp. 496–504.

Schütze, H. (1993). Word space. In *Advances in Neural Information Processing Systems 5*. Citeseer.

Traxler, M. J., M. J. Pickering, and B. McElree (2002). Coercion in sentence processing: evidence from eye-movements and self-paced reading. *Journal of Memory and Language 47*, 530–547.

Turney, P. D. and P. Pantel (2010). From Frequency to Meaning: Vector Space Models of Semantics. *Journal of Artificial Intelligence Research 37*, 141–188.

AUTHOR INDEX